Paris Metro Ha

D1512816

Brian Hardy

Capital Transport

Author's Note

It is now some six years since the second edition of Paris Métro Handbook was published. In that time and in true French tradition, there have been many changes. This new edition incorporates those changes and includes details of the new trains now in service, an extension of line 13 to Saint-Denis – Université, and the opening of the first stage of the new Météor line (line 14).

During the six-year period, the Métro has seen the demise of the articulated trains of 1952–53 and the first generation of rubber-tyred trains of 1956–57, which were the last to survive in the old colours. In 1994 the production version of the 'BOA' took over service on line 7bis and from 1997 new rubber tyred trains of MP89 stock began working on line 1. A fully-automatic version of these trains, with no staff on board, was provided for line 14 (Météor) which opened in October 1998. Plans are advancing for a new generation of steel-wheel on steel-rail rolling stock, dubbed MF2000, to replace some of the MF67 trains which are now 25–30 years old. Meanwhile, some of these trains have been refurbished (lines 3bis and 9), along with further trains of MP59 stock, and in the autumn of 1998 refurbishment of the rubber-tyred trains of MP73 stock began. With the French politicians and authorities devoted to public transport, the Métro operates a service to be envied by many. Celebrating its centenary in July 2000, the Métro's wing of the RATP is well equipped to serve its passengers in the new Millennium.

In preparing this edition, I wish to express my thanks to Brian Patton, who continues to translate various documents from French into English, and Bert Steinkamp who has shared his detailed knowledge of over 40 years. In Paris, the enthusiasm of Julian Pepinster has resulted in the gathering of much information and photographs and is greatly appreciated. However, without the help and encouragement from the Paris Transport Authority (RATP) this work would not have been possible – their patience and willingness to provide information and answers to what must have seemed never ending questions is gratefully acknowledged. A special note of thanks must go to the RATP's photographic library and to Serge Sampeur, who has not only continued to show me around the network, but made numerous documents and facilities available to me. Finally, special thanks are due to my wife Jeanne Hardy for typing the script and checking the final result. The information in this book is correct to January 1999 but it has been possible to update the rolling stock data to 31 March 1999.

Ickenham, Middlesex, June 1999   BRIAN HARDY

Third edition 1999

ISBN 1 85414 212 7

Published by Capital Transport Publishing
38 Long Elmes, Harrow Weald, Middlesex

Printed by CS Graphics, Singapore

Front cover Apart from trains in special advertising liveries, all Métro rolling stock in passenger service is now in the new RATP house colours of jade green and white. Lines 7 and 8 were the first to receive the new livery, both on MF77 stock. On line 8, a five-car train arrives at the southern terminus of Créteil – Préfecture on 27 July 1997. Plans are now being drawn up for the refurbishment of this stock, now over 20 years old. *Brian Hardy*

Right An artist's impression (aided by computer) of how the five-car MF2000 stock will look. It is interesting to note that the backdrop for the station décor is the very successful Motte-Andreu style of 1974–1983. *RATP (MF2000 Team)*

Contents

Lines 2 and 3 are parallel to each other at Villiers, but the platforms on the latter had to be built at a lower level because the line would eventually pass under the former, west of the station. This is the station under construction on 2 June 1902 with line 2 (left) and line 3 (right), showing the tunnel roof at the same height but the track formation at a lower level. This is very noticeable at today's station. *RATP*

CHAPTER 1

The Origins of the Métro

The first official mention of the idea of an urban métro in Paris was made in the convention signed on 31 May 1865 between the government and the Chemins de Fer de l'Ouest (Western Railways) concerning the working of the Petite Ceinture (Rive Gauche) railway line. A clause provided for the reversion of the conssesion to the government 'en prévision de l'exécution éventuelle d'un chemin de fer métropolitain ...' ('in the event of the possible future construction of a metropolitan railway ...'). This right was not in fact exercised. A law of the same year (Loi de 12 Juillet 1865) gave local authorities all over France the power to build railways 'd'intérêt local' (of local importance).

More serious consideration was given to the idea after the chaos of the Franco-Prussian War (1870–71), the upheaval of the Paris Commune (1871) and the establishment of the Third Republic. In 1872, the council of the 'Département de la Seine' adopted a proposal for an urban network of two transversal lines and a circular line, using the powers of the Law of 1865, but this plan was refused by the Minister of Public Works in the following year. In its turn, the government, mindful of the possible strategic use of a metropolitan system in time of civil or external war, stated that it should be built as an extension of the main line network. These opposing views were to dominate all official thinking for the next 25 years. When a further law was passed in 1880, strengthening the powers of local authorities to build railways on their own land, the Département de la Seine was excluded from its operation, but that authority then handed over its plans to the City of Paris, which continued to support them enthusiastically. This change ensured, however, that any line constructed under the Law of 1880 would not be able to penetrate the urban area beyond the gates of Paris.

In 1883 the City produced another plan for an urban system of two lines, but again the government rejected it. In 1888, the civic authorities supported a plan devised by Jean-Baptiste Berlier for a tube line, to be worked by electricity, from Porte de Vincennes to Porte Dauphine, along most of the route of the present line 1. The sharp curves and steep gradients of this line made it the true precursor of the Métro, though it seems to have been envisaged as a tramway rather than a railway. When Berlier was unable to raise the necessary capital to build the line, the City added it to its own plans.

Argument might have gone on indefinitely had not the approach of the Universal Exhibition planned for 1900 concentrated the official mind wonderfully. On 22 November 1895, the government finally admitted defeat and the Minister of Public Works confirmed the legal authority of the City to build the lines, 'd'intérêt local', with a view to serving the exhibition sites. Definite plans were then drawn up by a municipal commission under the chairmanship of André Berthelot, a city councillor, and on 9 July 1897 the City formally adopted a plan for a network of six lines, of a total length of 65km, to be worked by electric traction. This was approved by the law of 30 March 1898. It had originally been planned that the lines should be of metre gauge and that carriages should be only 1.9m wide, but as a condition of government approval, standard gauge of 1435mm had to be adopted and the width of the carriages had to be increased to 2.4m. The loading gauge remained, however, too narrow to allow the passage of main line trains.

Work on line 1 began in November 1898 and went ahead rapidly. It had been hoped to use tunnelling shields for much of the line, but these proved to be ineffective and most of it was built either by opening out the roadway or by driving galleries forward from working shafts. For eighteen months, Parisians had to put up with considerable disruption. Much of the spoil was removed by water, for which purpose a few small side tunnels were driven down to the bank of the Seine. The Métro's first chief engineer, Fulgence Bienvenüe insisted that no trace of the works should remain after they were completed. There were some problems with sewers and drains and at Concorde the line had descended below the water table to pass under one of these, but there were no insurmountable problems. The safety record was good and there was only one major accident, a collapse of the workings at Étoile on 11 December 1899, which in the event proved to be more spectacular than serious.

After some weeks of test running, the line finally opened for traffic without ceremony at 13.00 on 19 July 1900. At first there was some hesitation on the part of the public about using the Métro, but, encouraged by the cool atmosphere in the stations during a stifling heatwave above ground, both Parisians and visitors soon took to the new form of transport and the number of passengers carried rose from 1.8 million in August to almost 4 million in December. Thus encouraged, the City pressed ahead with the building of new lines and the original network was completed more than a year ahead of schedule, in January 1910.

CHAPTER 2

The Development of the Métro Network

Line 1

The premier line of the Métro – its original line – is line 1, which was opened on 19 July 1900 from Porte de Vincennes to Porte Maillot, running roughly on an east to west axis. At both terminal stations, separate island platforms for arrival and departure were provided, being connected by a sharply-curved single-track loop, which avoided the need for trains to reverse. Apart from Bastille station, where the line crosses over the Saint-Martin canal, the line was built in tunnel. The western end of Bastille station has the sharpest curve on the whole of the Métro system used by passenger trains, at 40m radius. Operation remained unchanged until an extension was opened beyond the city boundary from Porte de Vincennes to Château de Vincennes on 24 March 1934. The old terminal station at Porte de Vincennes was retained for the extension but the layout was subsequently altered to have one track in each direction only, instead of two. For this reason, the present station has unusually 'wide' platforms, the extra space being built over the former track area. A westward extension was made to Pont de Neuilly on 29 April 1937 but prior to that, new platforms had been constructed at Porte Maillot and were brought into use on 15 November 1936 in anticipation of the extension. The new line dives down and passes under the old loop line at Porte Maillot, with the new station being a short distance west of it.

Then the busiest line on the Métro, the Classic stock was replaced by pneumatic-tyred trains, which made their debut on 30 May 1963. The changeover was completed by December 1964. Although line 11 had been converted to 'pneu' operation from 1957, line 1 was the first major Métro line to be so converted.

A further western extension to line 1 was opened on 1 April 1992, from Pont de Neuilly to La Défense, the latter (already being served by RER line A), being named 'Grande Arche de La Défense' from its opening and the RER station taking this name at the same time. On leaving Pont de Neuilly, the line rises sharply to the surface and runs in the middle of Route Nationale 14, crossing the River Seine. On the west side of the Pont de Neuilly, the line goes underground, where immediately the intermediate station of Esplanade de La Défense is situated. The line then continues underground in cut-and-cover tunnels, but on an uphill gradient to Grande Arche de La Défense, from where the trains continue on empty to reverse. This is necessary because the arrival and departure platforms are in completely separate locations, above the tracks of the RER on each side of the mezzanines.

The present length of line 1 is 16.6km (including 0.6km in the open) and in 1997 it was the Métro's second busiest line, carrying over 136.9 million passengers in that year.

The arrival platform (seen here) and the departure platforms on line 1 at Grande Arche de La Défense are separated by interchange facilities with the RER and the two Métro tracks are located over their platforms.
Brian Hardy

When a terminus, Porte de Vincennes on line 1 comprised separate island platforms for arrival and departure, with a track on each side of both. Now, a single platform suffices in each direction with the space formerly occupied by the redundant track part of the platform. This is a view of the wide eastbound platform with an unrefurbished train of MP59 stock in the erstwhile royal blue and white livery. *Brian Hardy*

The original terminus at Porte Maillot is still partly accessible from the main running lines of line 1. The arrival platform area has been converted into a reception area, complete with Sprague rolling stock. The former departure platform is still rail-connected and this shows one of the all-night Sprague rail tours in the early hours of 19 November 1989. *Brian Hardy*

Just over 2km of line 2 operates in the open on viaduct. A train of MF67E stock descends towards the tunnel with Jaurès station in the background. *Brian Hardy*

Line 2

Line 2 originally began as a shuttle from Étoile (now Charles de Gaulle – Étoile) to Porte Dauphine on 13 December 1900. The latter terminal station is similar to the original line 1 terminus at Porte Maillot, the arrival and departure platforms being connected by a sharply curved loop of 30m radius. The first part of the main portion of the line was opened from Étoile to Anvers on 7 October 1902, followed by the section onwards to Bagnolet (renamed Alexandre Dumas in 1970) on 31 January 1903. This latter section comprises 2.2km on viaduct with four elevated stations (Barbès – Rochechouart, La Chapelle, Stalingrad and Jaurès) and crosses the main line exits from Gare de l'Est and Gare du Nord. In the case of the latter (between Barbès – Rochechouart and Stalingrad) the lengthened SNCF platforms for Eurostar trains now finish under the Métro viaduct. The last section of line 2 onwards to Nation was completed on 2 April 1903 and the pattern of operation has remained unchanged since then. Most unusually, the terminal station at Nation was built on a passenger-carrying loop, one island platform serving arriving and departing trains. Line 2 was originally known as 2 Nord (North) until 14 October 1907, from when it became line 2. The entire length of the line is 12.3km and operates wholly within the city boundary.

On the west side of Villiers, this June 1991 view shows line 2 (left) and line 3 (right) diving down to pass under on the alignment to Porte de Champerret. *Julian Pepinster*

The three levels at Opéra, where lines 3, 7 and 8 cross, all underground. *Julian Pepinster*

Line 3

Rather oddly, line 3 was not the next Métro line to be opened (line 5 in fact got in before 3 and 4). Line 3 was inaugurated in stages, as follows:

Villiers to Père Lachaise	19 October 1904
Père Lachaise to Gambetta	25 January 1905
Villiers to Pèreire	23 May 1910
Péreire to Porte de Champerret	15 February 1911

This line was the first to open after the Couronnes disaster on line 2 (q.v. Rolling Stock) and it incorporated improved safety features devised in the light of experience gained from that. There was a system of emergency lighting for the tunnels, the wires for which were buried in the ballast, and the stations had improved emergency facilities. Villiers station was a terminus for just over five years and trains reversed via a loop, which was away from the subsequent alignment to Porte de Champerret. All that remains now is a pair of sidings beyond the station and until recently were used for instructional purposes for train drivers. The loop beyond the sidings, which pass under the Parc Monceau, was abandoned during the 1930s and offices were built in it. More recently, these too have been abandoned. Line 3 was further extended at the eastern side of the city from Gambetta to Porte des Lilas on 27 November 1921. It was extended in the western suburbs from Porte de Champerret to Pont de Levallois on 24 September 1937.

9

A view of the never opened station at Haxo, which is located between Porte des Lilas and Place des Fêtes. A number of trains from line 3 stable between Porte des Lilas and here. When this photograph was taken, on 26 October 1989, experiments were taking place with fully automatic trains for the future, for which additional equipment had been installed on the track.
Julian Pepinster

For over 30 years, line 3 continued to operate between Pont de Levallois and Porte des Lilas, with a terminal loop at the latter. However, in 1971 a major reorganisation of line 3, which had began in 1969, was completed. The section from Gambetta to Porte des Lilas became a self-contained branch (line 3bis) on 27 March 1971 in connection with the opening of an eastern extension from Gambetta to a new transport interchange complex at Gallieni on 2 April 1971. This new extension required the provision of 'through' platforms at Gambetta. Two new platforms were thus built just west of the original station and were even closer to the adjacent station, Martin Nadaud. The distance between the old station at Gambetta and Martin Nadaud had been, at 0.23 km, the shortest distance between any pair of Métro stations. The new arrangement saw the access via Martin Nadaud retained and its old platforms continue to serve as west-end access to the new Gambetta platforms. The old island platform at Gambetta in the Paris direction became the terminus for line 3bis, while the other (former arrival) platforms were demolished, but the careful observer will notice (just) the remains of old tiled walls of the station on leaving Gambetta heading towards Gallieni. Line connections continue to exist at Gambetta between the branch and the main line and some trains from line 3 are stabled at Porte des Lilas, running empty to and from Gambetta.

Line 3 was the first to receive modern steel-wheel-on-steel-rail trains from late-1967, but line 3bis continued to operate the old Classic stock until 2 July 1981. The main line is now 11.7km long and the branch 1.3km – all of it underground.

The section of line 3 between Gambetta and Porte des Lilas became a self-contained shuttle service in 1971, when line 3 was extended from the former to Gallieni. A train of MF67 stock awaits departure from Gallieni on 12 January 1999. New station signs in lower case lettering have been installed at this station. *Brian Hardy*

Line 4

The unexpected difficulties found in the construction of a tunnel under the River Seine meant that line 4 was, unusually, originally opened as two disconnected pieces. The northern section between Porte de Clignancourt and Châtelet was the first to open on 21 April 1908, while the southern section between Porte d'Orléans and Raspail followed on 30 October 1909. The two sections were finally connected on 9 January 1910 – both northern and southern terminal stations were provided with loops. The line has not been extended since then, despite a number of proposals being put forward over many years. However, a 330m-long deviation of the line was completed on 3 October 1977 in connection with a new station at Les Halles, 30m to the east, to make interchange with the enormous RER complex at Châtelet – les Halles much easier.

Conversion to pneumatic-tyred trains took place between October 1966 and July 1967. This line, 10.6km long and all underground, continues to be the busiest on the Métro, carrying over 137.35 million passengers in 1997.

New platforms were opened at Les Halles on a new deviation of line 4 in 1977 in connection with providing interchange facilities with the RER station at Châtelet – les Halles. An unrefurbished train of MP59 stock is seen at Les Halles on 7 October 1996 in the new RATP livery (top), while a refurbished train is seen (lower). Compare the front-end styles *Both photos Brian Hardy*

A southbound train of MF67F stock arrives at Quai de la Rapée (line 5) on 23 March 1999, having just passed over the Saint-Martin canal. *Brian Hardy*

Lines 5 and 6

The second Métro line to be opened was what is now known as line 6, from Étoile to Trocadéro, on 2 October 1900. This line was first known as line 2 Sud (South) and was extended from Trocadéro to Passy on 6 November 1903 and on to Place d'Italie on 24 April 1906. There it was soon joined by line 5, whose first section from Place d'Italie to Gare d'Orléans (now Gare d'Austerlitz) was opened on 2 June of the same year. Line 5 had originally been intended to run from the Gare de l'Est to the Pont d'Austerlitz but the line as built was diverted to the west to run via Quai de La Rapée (at that date known as Place Mazas and renamed Pont d'Austerlitz from 1907 to 1916). It was then decided that line 5 should incorporate the section on to Place d'Italie originally intended to have been part of line 2 Sud, and this was in fact the first portion to be opened. Line 5 was extended to Place Mazas on 14 July 1906, from which date a connecting shuttle service was provided to Gare de Lyon. From 1 August 1906 the shuttle was replaced with a through service but with trains having to reverse at Place Mazas to reach Gare de Lyon. When the northern extension to Lancry (now Jacques Bonsergent) was opened on 17 December 1906, the service to Gare de Lyon was abandoned, leaving this station rather isolated on line 1 until the RER was built some 70 years later. The abandoned section of line served, between 1937 and 1967, as the 'finance line' where a double-ended motor coach collected cash from stations to be taken to the Gare de Lyon. It still survives to transfer rolling stock between lines 1 and 5 and is also used for instructional purposes for train drivers.

Over half of line 6 runs in the open, much of it elevated on viaduct. The line therefore has several noticeable gradients, as illustrated here with a train of MP73 stock in blue and white livery approaching. *John Herting*

The use of Place d'Italie as a terminus for lines 2 Sud and 5 was inconvenient for both operating staff and passengers and on 14 October 1907 the lines were amalgamated under the latter number. From the same date, line 2 Nord became line 2. A northward extension to Gare du Nord, situated on a loop, followed on 15 November 1907, after which the service remained unchanged for many years, save for the period from 17 May to 6 December 1931 when, during the Colonial Exhibition, it was curtailed to run from Place d'Italie to Gare du Nord.

The CMP was not particularly enthusiastic about line 6 in the early days, as it did not promise to generate much traffic and, though the infrastructure was completed by the City from Place d'Italie through to Nation in 1906, the Company took refuge in a clause in the original agreement which said that the lines should be opened in the order they were listed therein and consequently they did not begin to operate line 6 until after the first section of line 4 had been put into service. The actual opening date was 1 March 1909. The line was briefly extended to Étoile in 1931 in place of line 5 (q.v. above).

An extension of line 5 from Gare du Nord to Église de Pantin was under construction in 1939 but the opening was delayed by the outbreak of the Second World War and it was not until 6 October 1942 that new platforms were opened at Gare du Nord on the alignment of the extension. The extension itself was brought into operation on 12 October 1942. As line 5 would then have been too long for reasonable operation (between Étoile and Église de Pantin via Place d'Italie), it was, from the same date, curtailed to terminate at Place d'Italie. The section between Place d'Italie and Étoile was transferred to line 6, also on 12 October 1942, and this line described a southern arc of the City. Part of the former line 5 terminal loop at Gare du Nord is now used for driver training.

Much of line 6 is in the open air – in stark contrast to other early Métro lines. Some 6.1km of the 13.6km route length is on viaduct. Line 5 is mostly in the open air from north of Campo-Formio to just beyond Quai de la Rapée and this section is most interesting to the enthusiast. Climbing onto an elevated structure, the station of Gare d'Austerlitz is located in the roof of the main line railway station. The line then crosses the River Seine on the Austerlitz bridge before curving and descending sharply into tunnel, in which the connection to and from Gare de Lyon on line 1 is situated, then rising again to the surface at Quai de la Rapée. Not surprisingly, this section of line has earned the title of 'the toboggan'. On leaving Quai de la Rapée, the line immediately crosses over the Saint-Martin canal and then continues underground.

Line 6 was converted for pneumatic-tyred trains between October 1972 and May 1974. In comparison to other 'pneu' conversions, line 6 was undertaken mainly for environmental reasons, to reduce noise levels on the open sections of the line. The rolling stock was changed over from July 1974.

After over 40 years of unchanged operation, line 5 was extended from Église de Pantin to Bobigny – Pablo Picasso, opening on 25 April 1985, with one intermediate station at Bobigny Pantin – Raymond Queneau. This increased the length of line 5 from 11.2km to 14.6km. Among the problems encountered with the construction of this extension was severe flooding on 6 June 1982, caused by heavy thunderstorms and rain water subsequently building up in the new workings north-east of Église de Pantin station beyond the stabling sidings. The water then burst through onto the existing Métro system and 18 trains that were stabled were severely damaged by the immense torrent of water. Some trains were derailed and all had to receive major workshop attention. On the new extension, the route crosses the Paris – Strasbourg main line and the Ourcq canal, both underground. Part of the line, between Bobigny Pantin and Bobigny – Pablo Picasso, is in the open air and stabling sidings were built on the north side of the line, which has accommodation for over two-thirds of the rolling stock for line 5. A maintenance depot was built later, opening in April 1988. This was also designed to accommodate and maintain the trams which operate at street level from Bobigny to Saint-Denis, when services commenced in 1992. The distance between the two Bobigny stations, at 2.43km, was then the longest interstation distance on the Métro network, but has now been surpassed by the Châtelet–Gare de Lyon section of new line 14.

Snow is a rare commodity in Paris but special measures have been incorporated on line 6 should there be any appreciable amounts. A light snowfall is evident in this view taken on 21 February 1996 with an approaching train of MP73 stock rounding the curve into Sèvres Lecourbe.
Julian Pepinster

Line 7

The history of line 7 is one of the most complex of any Métro line. It was originally intended that it should run from Opéra to a terminus in the north-east of the City, but the municipal authorities were unable to decide on the exact location of this terminus and in the end it was arranged that it should take the form of a large loop, which would incorporate all of the proposed stations. It was later decided to add a branch to Porte de la Villette. The presence of abandoned underground quarry workings under the Buttes Chaumont caused problems in the construction of the line in that area and the first section to be opened was in fact from Opéra to Porte de la Villette on 5 November 1910. The line from Louis Blanc to Pré-Saint-Gervais was added on 18 January 1911. This was the first 'branch' of the Métro in the true sense and trains ran round the loop in an anti-clockwise direction. The outbreak of the First World War in 1914 delayed the opening of an extension from Opéra to Palais Royal until 1 July 1916, although work on the stations had not been quite finished even then. Extensions onwards to Pont Marie followed on 16 April 1926, to Sully – Morland on 3 June 1930 and to Place Monge on 26 April 1931. The line south to Porte de Choisy had already been opened for traffic on 7 March 1930 and had been worked temporarily as an extension of line 10. It now assumed its intended role as part of line 7 and was extended to Porte d'Ivry, also on 26 April 1931. One of only two extensions to the Métro in the immediate post-war period took line 7 further south from Porte d'Ivry to Mairie d'Ivry on 1 May 1946.

At the northern end of line 7, the branch to Pré-Saint-Gervais became a self-contained service as line 7bis from 3 December 1967, to allow a more frequent service to operate to Porte de la Villette, on which section the traffic offering was much greater. Whilst the main line received new rolling stock from June 1971, branch line 7bis continued to operate Classic stock until July 1980. Five-car trains of MF67F stock took over on a temporary basis until replaced by four-car trains of MF67E stock in 1984. These were replaced by new three-car trains of MF88 stock from January 1994.

Although one of the Métro's longer lines for many years, a number of extensions have been made to line 7. In the north, a two-station extension from Porte de la Villette to Fort d'Aubervilliers was opened on 4 October 1979. At the southern end of the line, the first stage of a new branch reached Le Kremlin-Bicêtre on 10 December 1982 and although it was the intention to serve each branch with alternate trains, it was found necessary to operate a pattern in the evening peaks so that Mairie d'Ivry had two trains to Le Kremlin-Bicêtre's one, because of the uneven traffic flows. This situation was rectified when the ultimate southern terminus of Villejuif – Louis Aragon was reached on 28 February 1985. Trains were then able to serve the two southern branches alternately and indeed, both have identical running times from end to end. The final extension to line 7 was opened to the public on 6 May 1987, when it was extended one station to La Courneuve – 8 Mai 1945. With a total route length of 22.4km, line 7 is now the longest of all Métro lines and is the third busiest line, carrying over 108.5 million passengers in 1997. Line 7 also operates the most trains in service (64) at peak times. Both line 7 and branch line 7bis (3.1km) are wholly underground.

Cross-platform interchange is provided at Louis Blanc on lines 7 and 7bis. A train of MF77 stock is seen (left) on line 7 with a train of MF88 stock (right) on line 7bis.
Brian Hardy

A view looking westwards towards La Motte-Picquet from Champ de Mars disused station on line 8, taken on 14 September 1991. *Julian Pepinster*

Lines 8, 9 and 10

The history of these three lines is also rather complex, and as they were planned together, they will be dealt with as a group.

Line 8 was mentioned in the first plans, but only as a line which should be constructed at a later date (the 'additional network'). It was finally agreed in 1903 that it should be built from the Opéra to Auteuil, with a branch (line 8bis) to Porte de Sèvres (now Place Balard). However, before any work was done, the line became merged in a much grander scheme. In 1907 the municipal authorities adopted a plan for an additional network, to follow the construction of the main system. This plan included the first part of line 9 and also an inner circle, to run from Invalides to Invalides via the Boulevard Saint-Germain, Bastille, République and Opéra. Between République and Invalides this line would share the tracks of line 8 to which line 9 might also be added. It was also planned that line 8 would include a connection to line 9 at the southern end to allow trains on both lines to serve both termini. It was all a very far cry from the lines that were already in operation, with their simple end-to-end services. Fortunately, the City and the CMP later had second thoughts – perhaps someone came to London and had a close look at the complex workings of the Inner Circle! – the grand design was never put into operation. However, it did influence both the course of the lines under discussion and the layout of the tracks in various places, such as in the vicinity of Invalides stations, and it is therefore important to bear in mind what the original plans were.

Line 8 was inaugurated on 13 July 1913 when the section from Opéra to Beaugrenelle (named Charles Michels since 1945) was opened to traffic. It was extended to Porte d'Auteuil in the form of a one-way anti-clockwise loop on 30 September 1913. The eastern end was extended from Opéra to Richelieu – Drouot on 30 June 1928 and further to Porte de Charenton on 5 May 1931, just in time to serve the Colonial Exhibition which opened the following day and was held in a large area of the Bois de Vincennes. In 1937 there was a re-arrangement of the south-western end of the line, which was diverted at La Motte-Picquet – Grenelle and extended to Balard on 27 July, its previous operation to Porte d'Auteuil being taken over by line 10. A south-eastern extension was opened on 5 October 1942 from Porte de Charenton to Charenton – Écoles.

After a long period of stagnation on the Métro generally, line 8 was the first of several lines to be extended from the 1970s. Four separate stages took the line from Charenton – Écoles to Créteil – Préfecture, as follows:

Charenton – Écoles to Maisons-Alfort – Stade	19 September 1970
Maisons-Alfort – Stade to Maisons-Alfort – Les Juilliottes	27 April 1972
Maisons-Alfort – Les Juilliottes to Créteil – l'Echat	26 September 1973
Créteil – l'Echat to Créteil – Préfecture	10 September 1974

This differed from all previous extensions in that the distance between the stations was on average much greater (1km as against 0.5km) and also because for the first time a supplementary fare was levied for travel on it as proposed in the 1929 plans. Supplementary fares have, however, been discontinued since 1 November 1982. Much of the open-air section to Créteil is, unusually, built in the central reservation of a motorway and the space for three tracks has been provided throughout. Only on some of the route from Maisons-Alfort – les Juilliottes to Créteil – Préfecture has a third track actually been provided. The intention was to operate a semi-fast or skip-stop service but this has been deferred and the third track on the south-west side of the line is used for stabling trains. Line 8 is 22.1km long, and has 2.8km of open-air running. This includes a crossing of the River Marne between Charenton – Écoles and Alfort – École Vétérinaire, and from north of Créteil – l'Echat to the terminus.

Line 9 was originally seen as a branch of what was then line 2 Sud from Trocadéro to Porte de Saint-Cloud. In 1907, however, it was decided that it should be extended inwards to Opéra as an independent line. Then, for a brief period, it was envisaged that it would be worked as a branch of the proposed inner circle. Finally, it was evident that this would overload the circle and the line was constructed on its own. The location of the terminal sidings at Porte de Saint-Cloud caused problems and construction was not only delayed by the outbreak of war but also by a collapse of the workings at Place de l'Alma on 8 November 1915, and by the post-war financial troubles of the CMP. The first section, from Exelmans to Trocadéro, was therefore not opened to the public until 8 November 1922. It was extended inwards to Saint-Augustin on 27 May 1923, to Chaussée d'Antin on 3 June 1923 and outwards to Porte de Saint-Cloud from Exelmans on 29 September of the same year. When the last part of the line was opened, it was planned that for special events at what is now the Parc des Princes stadium, alternate trains would be diverted south of Jasmin onto what was then line 8 (now line 10) via the Auteuil loop to a 'special events only' station at Porte Molitor. The island platform was built at track level but no connection was made to street level when the project was abandoned, as it had then been decided to keep the operation of lines 8 and 9 quite separate. From Porte Molitor, trains would have returned to line 9 via a large loop near Porte de Saint-Cloud. This section of line is now used for stabling trains on line 9, being part of a very extensive network of tunnels in the area. Meanwhile, the station area at Porte Molitor is used for stabling trains on line 10. Another proposal for line 9 which was not carried out was for a branch line from Saint-Augustin to Place des Ternes on line 2. At the former, the present 'wide' platform in the eastbound direction remains as a relic of these plans and has been used, on occasions, for exhibition purposes A third track was originally laid, but was filled in during the 1960s.

In the inner area, lines 8 and 9 were extended together, but on separate tracks, to Richelieu – Drouot on 30 June 1928, this section being originally planned as part of the inner circle. From there, the tunnels for both lines, with separate tracks (and mostly on separate levels), were constructed onwards to République, but not without considerable opposition from property owners along the line of the Grands Boulevards. For this reason, line 9 was constructed beneath line 8 from Rue Montmartre (renamed Grands Boulevards in 1998) to Saint-Martin. Line 9 was extended further eastwards to Porte de Montreuil on 10 December 1933. The south-western terminus became Pont de Sèvres on 3 February 1934 and was in fact the very first Métro extension beyond the city boundary, while the final extension in the east to Mairie de Montreuil followed on 14 October 1937. The total length of line 9, at 19.6km, has been unchanged since that date and all of it operates underground. Line 9 was the last to operate the old Classic stock, the last train running on 16 April 1983.

When construction work began on line 10 in 1913, it was still envisaged that this line would ultimately form part of the proposed inner circle and it was not until 1922, by which time a large junction layout had been constructed at Invalides, that it was decided that it should instead be confined to the Left Bank of the River Seine. It was opened from Invalides to Croix Rouge (the latter station, situated between Sèvres – Babylone and Mabillon, is now closed) on 30 December 1923 and traffic levels were at first derisory, since their two termini were not very far apart and the intermediate stations served no recognisable flow of passengers. It was extended one station to Mabillon on 10 March 1925 and to Odéon on 14 February 1926. To work line 10 more economically, a series of motor coaches with driving cabs at both ends, capable of running singly, was placed into service from December 1926.

Until the southern extension to line 7 was complete, line 10 was extended to Place d'Italie on 15 February 1930 and to Porte de Choisy on 7 March 1931. These extensions brought it an increased but unbalanced traffic. When line 7 eventually reached the Left Bank, it assumed operation of the new section to Porte de Choisy and line 10 was diverted to a new terminus at Jussieu, which was reached on 26 April 1931.

With another fairly drastic re-arrangement, carried out between 26 and 29 July 1937, line 10 was extended at Duroc (using new platforms at that station) over a newly-built section of track to La Motte-Picquet – Grenelle, then by the tracks of the former line 8 to Porte d'Auteuil from Duroc. The section northwards from Duroc to Invalides was handed over to a newly built line 14. At the eastern end, line 10 was extended from Jussieu to Gare d'Austerlitz on 12 July 1939, a distance of 1.03km, making this the longest distance between any two stations on the Métro until the extensions of the 1970s. Nevertheless, this was still the longest distance on the Métro within the City boundary, until the opening of Météor (the present line 14) in 1998.

Line 10 was then to remain unaltered until the opening of a western extension to Boulogne – Jean Jaurès on 3 October 1980 and one station further west to Boulogne – Pont de Saint-Cloud on 2 October 1981. Initially, with the exception of the evening service, alternate trains continued to terminate at Porte d'Auteuil, giving the northern section of the one-way loop a through service into Paris. In the evenings on the reduced headways, all trains worked through to Boulogne and passengers for Paris had first to travel to Boulogne – Jean Jaurès and change trains there – cross-platform interchange is normally timetabled. In 1991 the Monday to Friday Boulogne service was improved, with two trains in three running through and every third continuing to terminate at Porte d'Auteuil. From 1994, however, all trains were scheduled to run through to Boulogne on a daily basis, apart from those entering or leaving service at Porte d'Auteuil. From the autumn of 1997 a further change was made, whereby trains leaving service after the peaks continued to Boulogne and returned empty to Porte d'Auteuil, having to reverse between Michel Ange Molitor and Chardon Lagache. Only the last two trains of the day now actually terminate at Porte d'Auteuil. The complete line 10 is underground and is 11.7km long.

Line 11

Compared with other Métro lines, the history of line 11 is simplicity itself. It was originally planned in 1922 and opened from Châtelet to Porte des Lilas on 28 April 1935 and one station further on to Mairie des Lilas on 17 February 1937. As it was built much later than the other lines, line 11 usually had to pass under these when it crossed them and in consequence, many of the stations were built with escalators.

Because of the resulting sharp curves and gradients, it was an ideal proving ground for the operation of pneumatic-tyred trains, which went into service from 13 November 1956, following an official inauguration on 8 November 1956. The new trains on this line gave a rather lively ride right to their end, the last running on 30 January 1999. The first trials of Automatic Train Operation in revenue service were also made on line 11 from September 1967 and following its success, the conversion of all its trains was completed by June 1969, the first line on the Métro to be so operated.

At a modest 6.3km in length and using four-car trains, line 11 takes just 15 minutes from one end to the other – all underground.

Line 12

Line 12 was originally line A of the Nord-Sud company and was planned as a tube from Montmartre to Montparnasse. A few preliminary soundings showed that this would be an impossible undertaking and when construction actually began in 1907, it was built as a conventional underground Métro. The workings ran into the same difficulties with the abandoned quarry workings as were found on line 7 of the CMP and they were further held up by a series of strikes and by the disastrous floods of January 1910. There was something of a race with the CMP who were then completing the equipping of line 7, and in the end, both lines were opened on the same day – 5 November 1910. The first section to open to traffic was from Porte de Versailles to Notre-Dame-de-Lorette and extensions northwards brought the line to Pigalle on 8 April 1911, Jules Joffrin on 31 October 1912 and Porte de la Chapelle on 23 August 1916. This last extension was opened despite a shortage of rolling stock, as the firm that was then building some additional trains was in that part of Northern France then occupied by the German army.

No further extensions were made to line 12 while the Nord-Sud retained its independence. In fact, the only extension to be made in CMP days was from Porte de Versailles to Mairie d'Issy on 24 March 1934, since when the operation of line 12 has not changed. Prior to the extension to Mairie d'Issy, a new station opened at Porte de Versailles on 1 January 1930, 100m to the south of the original station. The tiled walls of the original station can still be seen today. The complete 13.9km of line 12 is in tunnel.

Rue du Bac on line 12 was one of those stations modernised with panelling in the 1960s, but it needed to be modernised again in 1984 because of the deteriorating condition of the original tiles behind. In this view the panels have been removed and reveal its former Nord-Sud identity.
Brian Hardy

Lines 13 and 14

The second and, as events turned out, final Nord-Sud line was line 13 (line B), opened from Saint-Lazare to Porte de Saint-Ouen on 26 February 1911, followed on 20 January 1912 by a branch from La Fourche to Porte de Clichy, trains serving each destination alternately. The line served densely populated working class districts and soon built up a good level of traffic. However, there was not much demand for first class travel and in due course the first class trailer cars were converted to composite cars, in order to increase second class accommodation, the first such vehicles on either the Nord-Sud or CMP systems.

Line 14 was originally planned as line C of the Nord-Sud company, but it was not built as such. Construction did not begin until 1934, four years after the CMP absorbed the Nord-Sud, and line 14 came into service with the opening of the section from Porte de Vanves to Avenue de Maine (renamed Bienvenüe in 1942 and now Montparnasse – Bienvenüe) on 21 January 1937. Further new tunnels from the latter station to Duroc were opened on 27 July 1937, on which date the section of line 10 from Duroc to Invalides was handed over to the new line 14. The terminal working arrangements at Invalides required departing trains to traverse a large loop, before taking up normal running at the first station south – Varenne.

Trains of MF77 stock in their original livery pass immediately north of Malakoff – Rue Etienne Dolet station on line 13. On the left are the main line railway tracks from Montparnasse. When TGV services were introduced, a high retaining wall was erected, as can be seen. *Brian Hardy*

The main line was extended from Porte de Saint-Ouen to Carrefour Pleyel on 30 June 1952, one of only two such short extensions to the Métro in the early-post-war period, until the 'rebirth' of the Métro from the 1970s. The then new articulated MA51 stock operated on line 13 from 1952, until its transfer to line 10 in 1975–76.

One of the early plans for the Regional Express Métro (RER) envisaged a line linking Gare Montparnasse with Gare Saint-Lazare, but it was soon realised that such a link could be provided at a fraction of the cost by connecting lines 13 and 14 and operating them as a combined through service. This would relieve congestion at Saint-Lazare, which was then (and still is) the busiest Métro station, and would improve capacity on line 13 from there to the two northern branches. In addition, the expanding business centres between there and Montparnasse justified this new extension, but also allowed a 25–30% traffic easing on the very busy line 12 between these two points.

The route taken by the line 13–14 link from Saint-Lazare was via Miromesnil, at which location the new station was built under and at right angles to that on line 9, thence to Champs-Élysées-Clemenceau (providing interchange with line 1) and then to Invalides, where a new northbound platform was built – trains travelling south therefore no longer had to traverse the large loop, which was retained for train stabling purposes. The connection between lines 13 and 14 was actually achieved in three stages, as follows:

Saint-Lazare to Miromesnil	27 June 1973
Miromesnil to Champs-Élysées – Clemenceau	18 February 1975
Champs-Élysées – Clemenceau to Invalides	9 November 1976

When the last section was opened, the complete line became one line 13.

Not only were lines 13 and 14 joined in the centre of Paris, but extensions were being made at the northern and southern ends into the suburbs. Previously, on 20 May 1976, the northern end of the main line was extended from Carrefour Pleyel to Saint-Denis – Basilique, and on the same date that lines 13 and 14 merged, a southern extension was opened from Porte de Vanves to Châtillon – Montrouge, the last two stations on this section being in the open air.

Thus, by the construction of a mere 7km of new Métro line, a regional link across Paris was created, which filled several awkward gaps in the existing network and provided connections with ten other Métro lines. In 1978, line 13 was the first recipient of the new MF77 trains, the line being completely worked by this stock by late-1979.

The northern branch was extended from Porte de Clichy to Gabriel Péri (Asnières – Gennevilliers) on 9 May 1980, and a crossing of the River Seine is made in the open on viaduct between Mairie de Clichy and the new terminus. The old terminal loop at Porte de Clichy has been retained for the stabling of trains.

There are different operating patterns on line 13 according to the time of day. In off-peak periods, each northern destination is served alternately. In peak times, however, the service is operates in groups of five trains, running Gabriel Péri/Saint-Denis/Gabriel Péri/Saint-Denis/Saint-Denis, with the service interval on the common section (Châtillon to La Fourche) being 1 min 45 sec. This service, operative from 1994, replaced a previous operating pattern that saw two trains to Saint-Denis and one to Gabriel Péri and was brought about by increasing traffic on the latter service.

A further extension to line 13 opened on 25 May 1998, when it was extended 1.261km from Saint-Denis – Basilique (renamed Basilique de Saint-Denis) to Saint-Denis – Université. This opened up an improved transport link to the expanding Université and enabled a new transport interchange complex at the new station. Just prior to this, the 1976-built station, Saint-Denis – Porte de Paris was rebuilt and enlarged for the 1998 World Cup. In the long term, it is proposed that the branch of line 13 to Gabriel Péri will be taken over by the new Météor line, and will be extended to Port de Gennevilliers.

The distances on line 13 from Châtillon – Montrouge to the northern termini are 18.115km (Saint-Denis) and 14.77km (Gabriel Péri).

The Shuttle (La Navette) and Abandoned Sections

The First World War delayed completion of a number of lines authorised for construction in 1909–10, of which an extension of line 3 from Gambetta to Porte des Lilas was one. Although work began in 1912, the First World War delayed its construction, but the infrastructure was essentially complete by 1918. This included a pair of platforms at Porte des Lilas and a loop beyond the station.

The plans also included extending line 7 from Place des Fêtes to Porte des Lilas, returning from the latter to Pré-Saint-Gervais. This required a second pair of platforms at Porte des Lilas. The completion of this extension would have rendered the present section of one-way direct line from Place des Fêtes to Pré-Saint-Gervais redundant. In the outward direction, a single platform was built at Haxo, but no connections were made to street level.

Line 3 was the first to be handed over to the CMP and was equipped and opened from Gambetta to Porte des Lilas on 27 November 1921. Prior to that, the CMP had no enthusiasm for completing the extension of line 7 until the City of Paris contributed financially. Thus, the idea of extending line 7 as originally planned was abandoned, as it was deemed that line 3 was sufficient to serve the area. The CMP did relent, in part, and connected the two lines with a one-train shuttle service between Porte des Lilas and Pré-Saint-Gervais, opening on the same date as the line 3 extension. The southern track, from Place des Fêtes to Porte des Lilas via Haxo was thus never opened to passenger traffic. The lightly-used shuttle line, 767m long, was closed at the outbreak of the Second World War on 3 September 1939.

Since closure, the shuttle track has often been used for experimentation. In 1951, experiments with pneumatic-tyred trains began and from 13 April 1952 the public were allowed to use the single motor coach when it was running, between the hours of 13.30 and 19.30. No service was provided, however, when the coach was off for maintenance, which took place on a storage track at Porte des Lilas. Experiments with automatic train operation also took place on this line from 1951 onwards. Apart from staff, sightseers and school children, there was very little traffic. The line was closed again when the trials came to an end, by which time it was decided to convert a complete Métro line to pneumatic-tyred train operation, line 11 being the one chosen. The disused platforms at Porte des Lilas are occasionally used for filming, the 'original' style making it ideal to recreate the Métro of years gone by. The northern section of line, between Porte des Lilas and Haxo, is used for stabling trains from line 3 outside the peak periods, which run empty to and from Gambetta.

Other sections of the Métro that have been abandoned over the years include:

* Porte Maillot old platforms and loop on line 1.
* The connection between lines 1 and 2 at Étoile (points lifted at each end).
* The former loop line at Porte de Vincennes (line 1 – track lifted).
* Quai de la Rapée to Gare de Lyon (between lines 5 and 1).
* Gambetta (line 3) – the present public passageway between line 3bis and line 3 (inbound direction) was formerly a running tunnel, while the former outbound direction forms the connection between lines 3 and 3bis.
* The former loop line at Villiers (line 3 – track lifted).
* Les Halles (line 4) old station (track lifted and site rebuilt).
* Gare du Nord (line 5) old terminal station loop (part of track lifted).
* Between lines 5 and 6 at Place d'Italie (train cleaning machine subsequently installed.
* The connection between lines 10 and 7 between Maubert Mutualité and Place Monge.
* At Duroc (the old course of the original line 10 – track lifted).
* Invalides loop (the original line 14).

CHAPTER 3

Line 14 'Météor'

Unlike all other lines of the Métro, the second line 14 has had a very short history from first conception, to the opening for public service. When the first edition of the present book was written in 1988, the line was mentioned only as a possible future plan, yet in exactly ten years it has been planned, built and opened for traffic. This is no mean feat indeed and the result is something the RATP is justifiably proud. Because it is so different from anything that has gone before in such a large scale in Paris, it is worthy of a short chapter on its own. Despite being 'hi-tech', the RATP now wishes the new line to blend in with the rest of the network and do what it does best – carry passengers quickly and efficiently – and to that end; Météor is now plain and simple *Ligne 14*.

It was the first completely new line to be built since line 11 in 1935 and only the second post-war extension to the system which was not a prolongation of an existing line into the suburbs. The reasons for its construction were rather the need to relieve RER line A and to improve links between the central area, and the new developments to the south-eastern areas of Paris (Bercy and Tolbiac) which were areas previously occupied by now redundant railway land and run-down industrial enterprises. A new line serving the Gare de Lyon, served on the Métro only by line 1, would also end the relative isolation of that important main line terminus.

From its opening as a through route in 1977, line A of the RER was consistently under pressure, and by 1988, it was clear that even the advent of the modern SACEM signalling system was insufficient to cope with the passenger numbers. For some years, RATP engineers had been drawing up plans for a fully automatic Métro line, and in 1988 Paul Reverdy, Chief Executive of the authority, presented this idea to the government as a means of dealing with the problem of line A. To that end, the new line duplicates RER lines A and D between Châtelet and Gare de Lyon and having no intermediate station, now makes this the longest distance between two Métro stations at 2.784km.

Whilst line 14 was being built, train and other equipment testing was undertaken on a specially built test track on a disused part of the Petite Ceinture railway line near Maison Blanche, where the first train of MP89 stock for Météor is seen going through its paces. *Brian Hardy*

The only station not to have separate six-metre-wide platforms is at Gare de Lyon, where space constraints dictated an island platform nine metres wide. Despite being a highly automated railway, screens are provided telling passengers the time (in minutes away) of the approaching trains. *Brian Hardy*

On 7 February 1989 the then Prime Minister, Michel Rocard, announced the plans for the line as part of the five-year plan agreed between the government and the Île-de-France region. Météor, as it was then known, was thus born. There was some concern that the project might have to be delayed in favour of line E of the RER, but in the event the government, anxious to promote public transport, found sufficient funds to allow construction of both lines to go ahead simultaneously. An announcement to this effect was made in October 1989. A declaration of public utility followed in May 1991 and in October of the same year, the board of RATP approved the outline plans.

The first optimistic forecasts had suggested an opening date in 1996 for a line between Maison-Blanche and Saint-Lazare, at a cost of 4.4 milliard francs, but the plans actually approved subsequently scaled the length down to the section between Madeleine and what was then known as Tolbiac – Masséna and increased the budget to 5.75 milliard francs.

Construction began early in 1992 and it was very soon evident that the date for the opening of the line would have to be revised. In 1993 it was stated that it would be in operation in time for the World Cup traffic in the summer of 1998, but in the event it proved impossible to maintain this deadline and RATP services had to cope with the traffic without the aid of Météor. However, almost all of the civil engineering was completed by the end of 1996 and trial running began in June 1997. The line was opened by President Jacques Chirac on 15 October 1998.

The final cost for the 7.1km length of the first stage of line 14 was 6.1 milliard francs. Of this, 30% came from the central government, 18.3% from RATP through a low interest loan, and the balance of the funding for the section from Gare de Lyon to Bibliothèque – François Mittérrand from the Region and City of Paris.

25

A staircase separates a pair of O&K escalators leading to the island platform at Gare de Lyon on line 14. Note the mostly concealed 'spiders web' form of station lighting. *Capital Transport*

A view of the platform edge doors employed at all stations on line 14, looking through to the tropical rain forest display in the non-public area at Gare de Lyon, where heavy rain storms occur at regular intervals! Should the train not be in alignment with the platform doors, it is possible to exit in an emergency by operating push-bar doors. *Capital Transport*

Météor begins in the 13th district, in the south-eastern part of the city, an area not previously well served by the Métro. The terminus, originally known as ZAC de Tolbiac (ZAC is an abbreviation for an Urban Development Zone), opened as Bibliothèque – François Mitterrand. It serves a new development and has interchange with RER line C, whose present station of Boulevard Masséna will being relocated to provide this – all trains on line C will ultimately serve Masséna on completion of the new interchange in September 2000.

From Bibliothèque the new line runs via a new station, Dijon (opened as Cour Saint-Émilion), to Gare de Lyon where there is interchange with Métro line 1 and lines A and D of the RER, as well as other SNCF suburban and main line services. The next station is Châtelet, where there is interchange with lines 1, 4, 7 and 11 and RER lines A, B and D. From there, Météor runs to Pyramides, to connect again with line 7, and on to a provisional terminus at Madeleine (interchange with lines 8 and 12).

In the summer of 1998, work began on the short 0.760km extension from Madeleine to Saint-Lazare, which will then offer interchange with Métro lines 3, 12 and 13, SNCF suburban and main line services, as well as RER line E (Éole) the first stage of which was expected to open in July 1999. The section of line between Madeleine and Saint-Lazare was dropped from the first stage of construction because of financial constraints. Opening is anticipated in 2003, for which two additional trains will be required.

Platform edge doors at all line 14 stations have the circular 'hoops' at intervals as part of their integral construction. This is the current southern terminus of the line at Bibliothèque – François Mitterrand. *Capital Transport*

Looking forward on an MP89 train on line 14. The (emergency) driving equipment is located in a locked cabinet beneath the front window. Otherwise, passengers can have a totally unrestricted view of the route along the tunnels. *Capital Transport*

However, extensions at both northern and southern ends of the line are already planned. From Saint-Lazare the line will be extended to pick up the branch of line 13 west of La Fourche and run to Asnières-Gennevilliers (Gabriel Péri) and thence to Port de Gennevilliers docks on the River Seine. In the south Météor will be extended to Olympiades in 2005 and onwards to Maison Blanche. Long-term plans see Météor take over the Villejuif branch of line 7 and go onwards to Orly Airport. Once complete, line 14 would be some 26km long.

Météor differs in several important respects from the other lines of the Métro network. Operation is entirely automatic and trains do not have driving cabs. The platforms are enclosed from the tracks by glass partitions, with sliding doors to give access to the trains as on the VAL line in Lille or on the Singapore Metro. The average distance between stations, 2km, is greater than on the present lines, (500m – 700m), allowing a service speed of 40km/hour against 25km/hour, which in turn increases line capacity. When in full operation, with eight coach trains, Météor will be able to carry 40,000 passengers per hour, an increase of 33% over the conventional system. At first, however, trains are formed of six coaches. In tunnels a walkway has been provided to allow passengers to evacuate trains easily in an emergency and all stations are fully accessible to passengers who have problems of mobility or who are encumbered by heavy luggage. The extent of interchange facilities is noteworthy, all stations on the initial stretch except Cour Saint-Émilion having connections with at least one other line, and these opportunities will greatly speed up the journeys of many passengers.

Prior to opening, it was envisaged that much of the passenger traffic on line 14 would come from Line A of the RER, which should be relieved of about 12,000 passengers per hour over the section Gare de Lyon to Châtelet during the peak period. A more striking improvement in service will occur when Météor is eventually extended over the branch of line 13, at present one of the most overcrowded sections of the Métro, with standing loads in the evening peak of five passengers per square metre. Météor will allow a service of 40 trains per hour on the branch in place of the present 12 and this in turn will allow an increase of capacity of 50% on the Saint-Denis section of line 13.

The first stage of line 14 provides a 2-minute service at peak times, requiring 13 trains in service plus one spare available at each end of the line. This provides a capacity of 25,000 passengers per hour in each direction with a commercial speed of 40 kph.

With no train staff needed, the service can adapt instantly to demand with additional trains being provided in the case of special events. This is particularly useful with special events at the 'Palais Omnisports de Bercy', where additional trains can be pressed into service in normal off-peak times from the terminal stations at a moment's notice.

We have already seen that whilst the rubber-tyred trains introduced from 1957 to 1974 were an unqualified success, but the time taken to convert the track and introduce the trains was a time-consuming business, and could be as much as 4–5 years per line on the longer Métro lines. Because of that, further conversions were abandoned. But the success of the principle meant that *new* lines could be built for rubber-tyred train operation which was, of course, adopted for Météor.

Whilst the new line has its own workshop at Tolbiac Nationale, major maintenance is undertaken at Fontenay depot on line 1. To provide access to the rest of the system, a connection with line 6 is provided at Bercy – trains proceeding to Fontenay cross over to line 1 at Nation.

All line 14 platforms have been constructed to ultimately take eight-car train lengths and all side platforms are a spacious six metres wide in anticipation of the large volumes of people expected to use the line. Note the suspended TV screen in the background which lists the time in minutes of the arrival of the approaching trains. *Capital Transport*

Above One of the concepts of Météor was 'access for all' and to that end, lifts have been provided from street level right down to platform level at all line 14 stations, although a change of lift is often necessary. This is a view of the lift from street level which leads to the ticket hall below at Bercy station. *Brian Hardy*

After experiments, the ticket offices on line 14 are more spacious and customer friendly than those on the rest of the Métro network, much use being made of glass. This is the new office on line 14 at Madeleine. *Capital Transport*

The initial plans for stations were intended to emphasise the relationship between the Métro and the urban areas above and would have included a viaduct crossing of the Seine and shafts to bring daylight into the heart of a station. Budgetary constraints have meant that such interesting ideas have not been carried through, but nevertheless the architecture of the stations represent a complete break with tradition and is based on the principle that stations are themselves buildings and not simply a collection of corridors. The ticket halls are wide and contain not only ticket windows and machines but also telephones and (at a later date) bank cash machines. Passengers then proceed to a mezzanine which leads down to the platforms. These are embellished with metal arcs, which contain the access doors to the trains. The station at Bibliothèque – François Mitterrand has been built in conjunction with redevelopment of the surrounding area and is a 'showpiece' station built near the National Library. The station is monumental in style, reminiscent of a cathedral, with stone pillars and walls of polished concrete. The unopened amphitheatre will come into its own when direct interchange with R.E.R. line C is completed in September 2000.

At all stations the lighting is arranged in BOA-like fittings, while at platform level, much of the lighting is concealed and is reflected upwards to give a soft and soothing effect.

The fully automatic line 14 has been equipped with an Automatic Train Operating System – ATOS – which has been developed by Matra Transport. The system controls train running, station stops and train/platform door opening. It also governs the safe operating speed of the trains and traction power, as well as responding to passenger alarms which, when operated, activates video recording equipment in the carriage concerned. In the event of a train not aligning up with the platform doors, it is possible for passengers to exit operating manual push-bars. Although the trains are currently six-cars long, with the extensions planned for the future, all stations on the initial stage have been built for eight-car trains, the platform screen doors at the seventh and eighth positions being locked closed.

Prior to the opening of line 14, because the idea of no-person-operated trains on the Métro had not been fully tested, it was necessary to build a test centre on which to prove the new technology. To that end, the RATP constructed a section of 'pneu' track in the 13th 'arrondissement' west of Maison Blanche. Part of the SNCF-owned but disused Petite Ceinture railway line served as the location for this one-kilometre-long test bed. The 'station' in the centre comprised a loop line and a 300m-long siding. The tests included Automatic Train Operation, platform/train door operation, in-car CCTV and video and the interface and operation with the control centre. The first two trains were delivered to the test track in the summer of 1995 and test running began in July of that year. The first train was delivered to line 14 in March 1997 and testing on the line began in June 1997.

The station lighting on line 14 is mostly 'concealed' with much use being made of reflective light, as seen here at Châtelet, which gives a very restful environment. Escalator sides and intermediate panelling are made of glass. *Capital Transport*

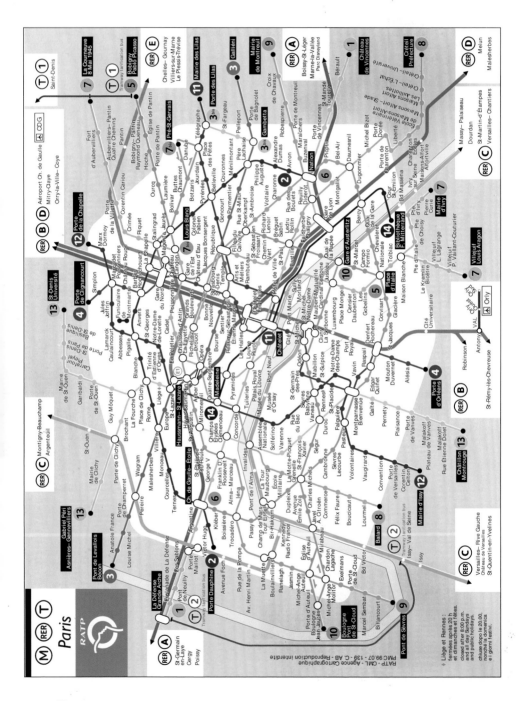

Possible Métro Extensions

The current ultimate aims for line 14 are to serve the area of Gennevilliers in the north and be extended to Orly Airport in the south. The current financial climate, however, probably precludes these plans being realised in their entirety in the foreseeable future. The northern extension would involve new tunnels from Saint-Lazare to join up and take over the present Clichy branch of line 13. Beyond the present terminus at Gabriel Péri, a new section of line would be built to Port de Gennevilliers, and a new depot would be constructed. The southern extension would probably take over the Villejuif branch of the present line 7 and ultimately be extended to Orly Airport.

Other extensions to the Métro system under serious consideration are as follows:

- Line 1 from La Défense to Nanterre – La Folie.
- Line 4 from Porte d'Orléans to Petit Bagneux.
- Line 7 from La Courneuve to Le Bourget.
- Line 9 from Mairie de Montreuil to Montreuil – Murs.
- Line 11 from Mairie des Lilas to Rosny – La-Boissière.
- Line 12 from Porte de la Chapelle to La Courneuve – Aubervilliers.
- Line 13 from Saint-Denis – Université to Stains – Moulin Neuf.

The regional council of Île de France also favour another automatic line from Austerlitz via Gare de Lyon to Villetaneuse along with a possible branch to Nation. In the 19th and 20th arrondissements this might use some of the trackbed of the Petite Ceinture railway line. However, the RATP has yet to adopt this idea.

Line Statistics

Line	Length (km)	Tunnel (km)	Open air (km)	Passengers (millions) 1997*	Stations Served (total)	Interchange Stations*	Open-air Stations
1	16.6	16.0	0.6	136.90	25	13	1
2	12.3	10.1	2.2	78.58	25	11	4
3	11.7	11.7	—	83.59	25	10	—
3bis	1.3	1.3	—	1.97	4	2	—
4	10.6	10.6	—	137.35	26	13	—
5	14.6	12.1	2.5	72.29	22	9	2
6	13.6	7.5	6.1	86.32	28	11	13
7	22.4	22.4	—	108.56	38	10	—
7bis	3.1	3.1	—	3.73	8	3	—
8	22.1	19.3	2.8	79.23	37	13	3
9	19.6	19.6	—	104.57	37	16	—
10	11.7	11.7	—	37.91	23	10	—
11	6.3	6.3	—	35.07	12	7	—
12	13.9	13.9	—	64.60	28	8	—
13	22.3	19.9	2.4	85.28	30	9	2
14	7.1	7.1	—	—	7	6	—

* Numbers include Métro and R.E.R.

CHAPTER 4

Stations

Original Design and Presentation

The original stations of the CMP possessed a unity of style, which apart from reducing construction costs, would have delighted any design consultant, had there been such around in the early 1900s. The walls were lined with white tiles, relieved only by the station names which were white on a blue ground, in either tiled form or on plates, by the maroon bench seats and by advertisements, though in the general gloom these would not have been much noticed. Some of the tiles on the original stations on line 1 and the first stage of line 2 were flat in finish, but subsequent tiles were of the bevelled type, which can be seen at numerous stations to this day. Only Porte Dauphine remains with the original style flat tiles on display, although they may be glimpsed at a few other stations which have had a partial refurbishment, for example at Porte de Vincennes. The platforms of Victor Hugo on line 2 were rebuilt and lengthened in 1931 and the abandoned section on the sharp curve at the west end of the station retains the original tilework. However, much experimentation took place in the early days with station tiles. Porte Dauphine and Victor Hugo had large flat ceramic tiles, small flat ceramic tiles were used at Porte de Vincennes, large flat white glazed tiles at Tuileries and Champs-Élysées – Clemenceau and bevelled white ceramic tiles at Argentine. The bevelled tiles were quickly adopted because they were far superior to the others.

A view of Étoile (now Charles de Gaulle – Étoile) prior to being renamed and prior to the line being converted to rubber tyred train operation. This line 6 terminus comprises a single track but has separate platforms for boarding and alighting. Note the overhead wire, which provided emergency lighting to Sprague and engineers' trains, a system now discontinued and mostly removed. *RATP*

The only Métro station to retain much of its flat tiling is the terminus at Porte Dauphine on line 2, whose station name is one of many with a suffix. The advertisements have paper edging to give the impression of being tiles. *Julian Pepinster*

Louvre station on line 1, built by the cut-and-cover method as illustrated by the overhead girders, photographed on 15 November 1967 before renovation. *RATP*

All stations are able to accommodate a train length of five cars at least (75m), although some lines operate trains of shorter length. However, from 1928, the newly constructed stations on lines 1, 3, 7, 8 and 9 were built to a length of 105m in anticipation of seven-car trains at a later date, a plan which has never been implemented. More recently, the original stations on line 1 were lengthened from 75m to 90m between 1961–64 and on line 4 between 1964–67. This work was necessary because the trains were being increased from five- to six-cars, which coincided with the introduction of rubber-tyred trains on those lines.

Stations longer than the standard 75m length are summarised as follows:

Line	Approx Length (m)*	Stations
1	105	La Défense – Grande Arche, Porte Maillot to Pont de Neuilly, Hôtel de Ville, and Reuilly Diderot to Château de Vincennes.
1	90	Saint-Paul, Châtelet to Argentine and Esplanade de La Défense.
3	105	Gallieni and Porte de Bagnolet, Louise Michel to Pont de Levallois.
4	110	Les Halles, Saint-Michel and Cité.
4	90	All other stations on line 4.
5	90	Gare d'Austerlitz.
7	105	Sully – Morland to Maison Blanche and Porte d'Italie to Mairie d'Ivry.
8	105	Balard to La Motte-Picquet – Grenelle and Opéra to Maisons-Alfort – les Juilliottes.
9	105	Pont de Sèvres to Marcel Sembat, Miromesnil and Grands Boulevards to Mairie de Montreuil.
10	105	La Motte-Picquet – Grenelle (westbound).
13	90	Châtillon-Montrouge.

Note * Minor variations at some locations.

Significant differences to standard include:

Line 1 – Bastille (125m) and Gare de Lyon (123m). It is, however, doubtful if a seventh car could be accommodated at Bastille, because the additional length is on a sharp curve.

Line 2 – Victor Hugo (142m) with the 'old' (curved) section abandoned.

Line 3 – Gambetta (196m) includes platforms of former Martin Nadaud station.

Line 13 – Invalides (115m), Miromesnil (111m) and Mairie de Clichy (112m).

Line 14 – All stations built to accommodate eight-car trains.

Lighting was by clusters of incandescent lamps which were described as 'brilliant'. Having established these standards, the CMP then stuck to them for the first four decades of its existence. Although there was great consistency, stations that were built to the cut and cover method were instantly recognisable by the steel girders at roof level, whereas other stations had white tiles extended right over the station ceiling. It was not until 1937, by which time ideas of brilliance had obviously changed, that the first attempts were made to improve the lighting, mainly in those stations dealing with traffic to the international exhibition of that year. But, neither this nor the post-war experiments with fluorescent lighting, did anything for the general image of the Métro as conveyed to the public in its stations. It also did not help that the ticket collectors' booths and the ticket offices were painted dark green and cream.

In 1994/95, Nord-Sud stations on line 12 (Sèvres Babylone) and line 13 (Place de Clichy) were lovingly restored to original condition, complete with tiled station names and the tile pattern over the vault. The Nord-Sud used green tiles at terminal and interchange stations and brown tiles at others. This is Place de Clichy on 27 April 1994 soon after completion of the restoration work.
RATP

The Nord-Sud company had done rather better in its presentation of stations. The roofs were decorated with patterns of occasional green (at interchange and terminal stations) or brown tiles (at other stations) and the advertisement panels were similarly framed, with the company's N-S entwined logo incorporated in the design. Over the station tunnel mouths, similarly coloured tiles picked out the name of the terminal station or geographical area then in use. This accounts for some stations on line 12 having 'Direction Montmartre' or 'Direction Montparnasse' instead of Porte de Versailles or Porte de la Chapelle, the line having opened in stages. Another interesting feature of the Nord-Sud is the rotunda forming the ticket hall of Saint-Lazare, which is of considerable merit and has been retained. It is gratifying that the RATP has totally rebuilt two of these stations to their former glory, Place de Clichy on line 13 and Sèvres Babylone on line 12. On the other hand, three stations remain in near original condition (Solferino and Porte de la Chapelle on line 12 and La Fourche (lower level) on line 13), while Porte de Versailles (line 12) and Porte de Clichy (line 13) retain their Nord-Sud identity, but were modernised in the 1970s. Liège on line 13 was inexpensively 'restored' in the 1980s with city of Liège panels, making this a cultural station.

Saint-Martin station was one of many stations closed at the outbreak of the Second World War, having been opened only since 1933. This is a 1990 view of the eastbound platform on line 9, which is built under the platforms of line 8, hence the low roof.
Julian Pepinster

Station Closures

The First World War had a severe effect on Métro services, with stations and sections of line closed, and brought about a reduced traffic day on those that were open.

This began right at the start of mobilisation on 2 August 1914 when lines 2, 6 and 8 were closed in their entirety along with line 5 between Étoile and Place d'Italie and the Pré-Saint-Gervais loop of line 7. A total of 63 stations were thus closed. Lines remaining open were curtailed to operate between 07.30 and 19.30 only. A slight relaxation of the operational hours was made from 20 August 1914, with services beginning at 07.00 and ending at 20.30. At the same time the Pré-Saint-Gervais loop line was reopened, which was followed on 1 September 1914 with the Étoile – Place d'Italie section of line 5.

Other closed lines reopened on 18 October 1914 and the remaining stations that were closed reopened by 1 December 1914. The service operating hours were relaxed further from 31 January 1915 with services running between 06.00 and 23.00 and all stations open. However, your writer has no details of the sections of line and stations closed during this period on the two Nord-Sud lines.

The Métro system had grown to 159km at the beginning of September 1939. The start of the Second World War saw the system reduced in operational size to just over 92km, with only 85 stations open to the public. Some lines were closed completely, while many stations and sections of line were closed. Those lines and stations that were open had, for a short time, a 24-hour service to allow soldiers to be able to travel at any time to the main line railway stations.

Indeed, some stations encountered two or three periods of closure, but Saint-Sulpice on line 4 was closed on no fewer than four separate occasions. At the end of 1945 there were still 72 Métro stations closed, of which 43 reopened in 1946 and 13 more in 1947. A further seven were eventually reopened in 1951, but this left a further nine still outstanding:

Arsenal (line 5)	Champ de Mars (8)	Cluny (10)
Rennes (12)	Croix Rouge (10)	Liège (13)
Bel-Air (6)	Saint-Martin (8 & 9)	Varenne (14)

Over a decade followed before two further stations were reopened. These were Varenne (on 24 December 1962) and Bel-Air (on 7 January 1963). However, it was on 29 June 1967 that the fate of the eight remaining stations was decided by the RATP. Two were to reopen (Liège on 20 May 1968 and Rennes on 16 September 1968, both on Mondays to Saturdays only and until 20.00), but it was intended that the other six were to remain closed permanently. One subsequent exception to this was the station of Cluny, which later featured in plans to be linked to the Saint-Michel station complex serving RER lines B and C. It reopened on 17 February 1988, named Cluny – La Sorbonne. For a period of time before re-opening, Rennes was used for advertising projects, which could be observed from passing trains.

Post-War Station Presentation

In the early post-war years, it was recognised that the general appearance of stations was no longer in keeping with contemporary standards of design, but at first no money was available for general improvement, other than the installation of fluorescent lighting. After some unsuccessful experiments, this was developed to a reliable standard and was generally adopted in the 1950s.

The first complete rebuilding of stations was done on a very individualistic basis, the aim being to give each station its own atmosphere and to break totally with the unity of the past. Six stations were thus modernised between 1952 and 1958. The first to be so treated was Franklin D. Roosevelt on line 9, which in 1952 was completely refurbished using unpainted aluminium panelling and illuminated advertisements. This was followed in 1954 with stainless steel cladding for Opéra on line 3, while in 1955 Chaussée d'Antin (line 9) was modernised in a further different style, followed by Saint-Paul (line 1) in 1956. In 1957 the line 1 platforms at Franklin D. Roosevelt were refurbished in glass and aluminium, the remaining painted sections being rendered in orange-red and blue.

One of the station décor experiments of the 1950s included Chaussée d'Antin on line 9, seen in 1979 before further modernisation. New panels have been affixed to the original tiles, which remain underneath. *RATP*

The idea of erecting panels over original tiles was developed further and experiments took place at the closed Arsenal station on line 5. This view, on 23 October 1958, shows the style that was adopted during the 1960s, but with varying presentations for station names. Brown and cream name plates were eventually adopted. *RATP*

Between 1960 and 1965 a total of 69 stations were modernised with panelling covering the original tiles. Originally the panels were cream but they have been changed in recent years to be painted white. In addition to the standard fluorescent lighting, concealed lighting was also a feature of this style which illuminated the advertisements. Pop singer Céline Dion watches over proceedings at Marx Dormoy on line 12. *Brian Hardy*

The sixth and final experimental modernisation was carried out at République on line 3 in 1958, and with its orange coloured panels covering old tilework, this set the standard for future station modernisation on the Métro. Between 1960 and 1965, therefore, some 69 stations were renovated in a unified style, which allowed greater advertising space than hitherto. The money generated by the increased advertising was able to further finance the project. The walls were sheeted with metal panels painted a deep creamy-yellow with a green relief. The station seats were an almost continuous bench in either light or dark green or wooden finish, but not surprisingly these seats often attracted those more interested in sleeping than travelling, and in later years were cut down to form individual seats, while others were replaced. The station names and platform 'Direction' signs were picked out in cream on a brown background and, to the eyes of the British enthusiast, these stations had a distinct touch of Great Western Railway flavouring about them! The station ceilings were generally left with white tiling, or, in the case of cut and cover stations, left with the steel girders showing, but a small number of stations had the tiles removed on the vault and it was painted yellow or white. Unfortunately this modernisation reduced the available platform area and brought about increased problems of cleaning and maintenance of the original tilework behind. For these reasons the style was abandoned after 1965.

A number of the stations modernised in the 1960s had the narrow panels replaced by large sheet panelling in the 1990s. One such station is Anvers on line 2, where the new bright yellow colour scheme does much to enhance the finished product. *Jeanne Hardy*

The next style of renovation appeared in 1969, initially at Mouton-Duvernet on line 4 and the opportunity was seized to refurbish stations which most needed attention to the tilework. In this scheme, the old white tiles were removed completely and replaced by new flat yellow-orange tiles up to 2.20 metres high on platform side walls. This section of the platform wall, including the advertisement panels, was illuminated, but the main lighting was arranged in shaded 'blocks' along the platform edge. The roof of the station remained in shadow and the overall effect was rather gloomy compared to the previous style. A further variation in station name signs appeared with this style, being white on grey. These still remain at Commerce (line 8), La Motte-Picquet – Grenelle (line 8 – westbound) and on H-frame stands at Nation (line 6). The rest have been replaced by the standard white on blue nameplates and the individually-shaped group of bench seats have been replaced as well. A total of 21 stations were modernised to this design which acquired the name of 'Mouton-Duvernet' after the prototype. It was realised at an early stage that the finished product was 'not in accord with fashionable ideas'.

Between the various modernisation schemes, a number of experimental styles have been tried. At Odéon (line 10) and Rennes (line 12) the platform tiles were covered by plaster and the walls were painted in a very pale pink. Station names at Odéon comprised illuminated signs, red on pale pink. This work was done in 1967–68. Other experiments include Opéra (lines 7 and 8). Havre Caumartin (line 9), Pasteur (line 6), Nation (line 9) and Saint-Lazare (lines 12 and 13), all of which were really variations of the 'Mouton' style, done in the same period, 1973–74, but differed in the colour of tiles used. Other stations to follow a similar style to the Mouton group include Gambetta (the new station on line 3), and Kléber, both of which have bevelled fawn-coloured tiles. The new works which took place in the early–1970s were all of one general style. They included the extensions to Créteil (line 8), to Asnières, Saint-Denis and Châtillon (line 13), to Bobigny (line 5) and Villejuif (line 7). The tunnel stations are quite similar, having small tiles, and include the two new stations on line 13 (Miromesnil and Champs-Élysées – Clemenceau) and the modernised station at the former on line 9. Some of these stations now present a gloomy appearance in comparison with others.

The next modernisation scheme to evolve was from 1969, where platform tiles were replaced completely rather than being hid behind panels. The colour scheme was predominantly red and orange, as illustrated at Commerce on line 8, but the station roof was kept in darkness. This station, like Liège on line 13, comprises separate platforms for each direction, because the line follows the (narrow) street above.
Jeanne Hardy

From 1974 a completely new style was trialled, following which over 90 stations were so modernised into the 1980s. Individual colour co-ordinated schemes were employed for each station, which included station furniture and light fittings. At stations built by the cut-and-cover method, the same colours were also applied to the roof girders, as seen at Concorde on line 1. *Brian Hardy*

In 1973, therefore, a design panel was set up to advise on future station modernisation policy. Its main recommendation was that the vaulted roof of the station should become a focal point of the design, instead of being left in obscurity, and that it should be indirectly lit by sodium lamps. It was also suggested that white should remain as the predominant colour but that the tiles should be relieved by two bands of similar or matching colour, at the level of the seats and on the lighting strip over the edge of the platform. A new type of bucket seating (also in matching colours) was devised to replace the wooden benches and the various items of platform furniture were also regrouped to give an impression of visual unity, making the stations look tidier. Three stations were thus modernised as trials in 1974 and met with enthusiastic response from the public. The comments made, however, showed there was still some desire for variety. The three stations chosen for the trials were Pont Neuf (line 7), Ledru-Rollin (8) and Voltaire (9). In the general application to this scheme, therefore, six colours were chosen not only for variety, but to complement the luminosity of the sodium lighting. The colours were red, lemon yellow, dark blue, lime green, orange and light brown. The scheme has not been slavishly copied in every instance, but it has been varied where necessary to suit the characteristics of a particular station. At the original cut and cover stations, for instance, the overhead steel girders have been repainted in colours matching the station furniture. This is called the 'Motte-Andreu' style, after the name of the two designers.

This programme was halted in 1985, following cuts in spending within the RATP, but not before 93 stations had been modernised with this successful style. Many stations have been extensively modernised with completely new flat tiles, while 50 other stations still retain the old bevelled tiles, which have been replaced only where necessary. Some of the latter type of stations still retain tiled station names and original tiled advert surrounds, and all of the stations at first equipped with sodium lighting have been re-equipped with 'white' light.

Most of the tunnel stations built since the 1970s on the Métro are instantly recognisable as being cut and cover construction, with their rectangular boxed shape. A good deal of individuality has been shown in the design of these stations, with imagination used for lighting schemes and decoration.

Saint-Denis – Porte de Paris on line 13, which was opened in 1976, was enlarged and rebuilt during 1996–98 because of the World Cup Football Championships in 1998, that station being one of three that were close to the newly built Stade de France. Apart from platform redecoration, the ticket-hall area was doubled, additional stair access constructed and lifts installed. A total of five stairways give street access.

The reduction of money available to modernise stations meant less grandiose products in the mid-1980s, the result being minor station renovations but often 'individualised' with small themed displays. The chance was then taken to exploit the 1960–65 style, often by painting the creamy-yellow panels white and repainting the ducting into varying colour schemes.

The last station to remain in the 1960's colours of cream and brown was Saint-Sulpice on line 4. This was finally changed in 1995 when the panels were replaced and the ducting repainted. In fact, a total of 37 of the 1960's style platforms remain, but with white panels and repainted ducting. More recently the narrow horizontal panels have been replaced by large white sheet panelling at 26 stations.

In 1987 the RATP began a pilot scheme in station modernisation at Stalingrad on line 7. This comprised total renovation but more cost-effective techniques and materials were used than hitherto. The result was very pleasing, with the station lighting reflecting colours onto the white tiled ceiling, giving a 'rainbow' effect. A new style of station seat (for three passengers, each separated by solid armrests to deter sleeping vagrants) was adopted, along with lean-on perches, but many of these seats and perches have since been replaced because of fixing difficulties. To date, 27 stations have been so renovated, although four are without the 'rainbow' lighting. This style is called 'Oui-dire', which accords with the name of the design group.

The refurbishment at Rue du Bac completed in 1984 is now devoid of all its Nord-Sud identity (see page 20). This is one of just a few stations in this style to have had the tiles on the vault removed, plastered and painted. A feature of this style of modernisation is that lighting is additionally directed onto the vault. *Brian Hardy*

The 'Oui-dire' style was introduced in 1987, the first station to be completed being the prototype at Stalingrad on line 7. Since then a further 26 stations have been so modernised, with many of them having colours reflected onto the vault. A co-ordinated colour scheme is again employed, in this case yellow (for the light fittings, advert surrounds and station furniture). *Jeanne Hardy*

The same principles as applied to Château Landon on line 7, where a wall separates the platforms. Here, the main colour is red. *Jeanne Hardy*

Three of the elevated stations on line 6 have been recently updated, which includes new seating, light fittings and replacement of the tiles. At Quai de la Gare on 17 November 1998 much of the lighting is now concealed while the station seats have been positioned on tiled bases. *Jeanne Hardy*

An experiment was undertaken in 1997 to modernise a station to original style, but to improving the lighting. That chosen was Saint-Ambroise on line 9 and is seen on 26 July 1997. The new lighting is more 'restful' but old style features of Métro stations, such as tiled advert borders, tiled station names and the traditional bevelled tiles remain. Other stations are now being so treated. *Jeanne Hardy*

Gare d'Austerlitz on line 5 is unique, in that it is located in the roof of the main line railway station. This station was partially modernised in 1985 with new lighting and seats. *Jeanne Hardy*

One of the more unusual modernisation schemes was undertaken at Cité on line 4 in 1991. This station is located on the Île de la Cité and crosses under the River Seine on both sides. Note the high roof. Whilst some features from the Oui-dire style have been employed (seats and tiled advert surrounds), the unusual lighting makes this rather unique. *RATP*

Saint-Jacques on line 6 is one of only a few Métro stations to have a street-level entrance and ticket hall combined, retaining the ornate tiling and signs in this 1991 view. *RATP*

In addition to the many variations to station styles on the Métro, some of the specific themes at selected stations, mostly incorporated within a particular modernisation scheme, deserve a special mention. The first and perhaps the most famous station is Louvre – Rivoli on line 1, so completed in 1968 (when named Louvre) with replica exhibits from the nearby Louvre Museum, indirectly lit against a restful background of cream coloured stone. The number of stations with themes continues to increase and such stations include:

Line 11 ARTS ET MÉTIERS – Arts and crafts.

Line 12 ASSEMBLÉE NATIONALE – Renamed from Chambre des Députés in 1989. Large nameless silhouettes are the main theme on advert spaces in various colours, which illustrate the phrase above 'Wherever its members are gathered together, there is the National Assembly'.

Line 13 BASILIQUE DE SAINT-DENIS – Commemorates the Royal Basilica of Saint-Denis.

Line 1 BASTILLE – Commemorates the Bicentenary of the French Revolution.

Line 7bis BOLIVAR – A display about the work and life of Simon Bolivar.

Line 7 CHAUSSÉE D'ANTIN – A large painting covers all of the vault which is dedicated to La Fayette, the French hero of the American War of Independence, whose name now appears as a suffix on the platforms of lines 7 and 9. The work was sponsored by the nearby and famous department store 'Galéries Lafayette', and was completed in November 1989.

Line 9 CHAUSSÉE D'ANTIN – The vault mural depicts common images of France and America – sciences, cinema, literature, poets and music. Additional lighting has been deflected upwards to illustrate the work.

Line 10 CLUNY LA SORBONNE – Reopened in February 1988 after being closed for nearly 50 years, the station has mosaic tiles on the vault depicting birds and signatures of famous names connected with Sorbonne University and French history.

Line 12 CONCORDE – What might seem an oversize 'Scrabble' board, the theme is an alphabetical puzzle on the Rights of Man and the Citizen. It goes without saying that the 44,000 ceramic tiles had to be carefully applied! Seats akin to those found in parks and city squares have been installed.

Line 13 LIEGE – Kept to Nord-Sud style, with murals relating to this Belgian city.

Line 6 MONTPARNASSE-BIENVENÜE – Photographic section on eastbound platform showing development of Métro in honour of Fulgence Bienvenüe, the 'Father of the Métro'.

Line 3 PARMENTIER – An agricultural theme, with the potato given prominence.

Line 5 PORTE DE PANTIN – Completed in November 1989, the station also gained the suffix 'Parc de la Villette'. The tiled walls comprise coloured musical 'note' symbols on a white background. The station ceiling originally in dark blue had a laser installed to show motifs. With the new style seating and diffused lighting, it is said to create the atmosphere of a music hall!

Line 7 PONT NEUF – Completed in December 1989 with the suffix 'La Monnaie', its theme is related to the Museum of the Mint opposite the station. Large replica coins and medallions adorn the station vault.

Line 13 VARENNE – This station is near to the Rodin Museum. Replica statues can be seen on the southbound island platform.

Line 2 VICTOR HUGO – Displays commemorating the work of this famous writer.

It should also be noted that many other stations have small displays of varying subjects, often of local interest, but are too numerous to be listed individually.

One of the more unusual cultural station refurbishment projects was undertaken at Arts et Métiers on line 11. It appears to represent the engine room of a ship, with the portholes along the platforms containing small themed displays.
Jeanne Hardy

The platforms of line 1 at Bastille were refurbished in 1989 to commemorate the Bicentenary of the French Revolution.
RATP

The Rights of Man is the theme at Concorde on line 12, which must have been a nightmare for those installing the tiles, ensuring all the letters were put in the correct place. The seats are replicas of those often found in public parks and gardens.
Jeanne Hardy

In 1968 Louvre was the first Métro station to become culturally decorated, with replica exhibits from the nearby Louvre Museum. The station was renamed Louvre – Rivoli in October 1989 because direct access to the Louvre Museum became available at the adjacent station, Palais Royal. *Brian Hardy, Capital Transport*

Chambre des Députés was renamed Assemblée Nationale in June 1989 and this view, taken on 21 January 1990, shows the replacement names taken down and the original Nord-Sud style names on the walls, at the earliest stages of station refurbishment. *Julian Pepinster*

The scheme adopted for Assemblée Nationale used large nameless silhouettes along the platforms. *Brian Hardy*

The stations on the new line 14 (Météor) offer a totally different environment from that which has gone previously. Spacious platform areas and passageways are illuminated discreetly, with much concealed lighting. Platform edge doors add to passenger safety and prevent service disruptions. All seven stations have a common style but each has its own individual finish. Bibliothèque – François Mitterrand, for example, is like a 'cathedral' with its lofty ceiling and has an 'amphitheatre' which will be fully available when the interchange with RER line C is complete. The present northern terminus at Madeleine has a circular interchange shaft in artificial light, giving a daylight effect, with escalators criss-crossing between the lower and upper levels.

Perhaps the most unusual and imaginative station on line 14 is Gare de Lyon, the only island platform station on the line. With the tracks on either side, the platform here is 9m wide (the single side platforms at other stations are all 6m wide), having to be squeezed in the space between Gare de Lyon main line station and the RATP headquarters building. At platform level, the space was originally to have been a connection with the Métro exhibition of a proposed transport museum, but cost-cutting saw this project abandoned. In its place, a 'tropical rain forest' has been created with 'rainstorms' programmed every two hours, although exactly when has so far eluded your writer! This idea was copied from the Atocha main line station in Madrid.

The cathedral-like proportions of Bibliothèque – François Mitterrand station can be appreciated here. Out of the picture on the left is an 'amphitheatre' which will come into its own when interchange with RER line C is completed in September 2000. *Capital Transport*

Stations for the New Millennium

With some of the Métro system being a century old, the RATP has recognised that some stations are showing signs of ageing. To remedy that, a plan to modernise nearly 200 stations (the Métro Renewal Programme) has been announced, which will involve new lighting, tiles, ceilings and signs. This will not only include the platforms but other areas of the stations as well. In the first stage of this programme, a total of eight Métro stations (and one RER station) are being renovated with various cultural themes for the occasion. These are:

Tuileries (line 1). This station will reflect the heritage of the RATP and will have some 480 illustrations on the theme of 'I remember', in six specific periods, which will be changed regularly to intrigue the passenger. There will also be a wall magazine which will be changed every three months and will cover topics such as rolling stock and tickets. A boutique 'The Heritage of the Métro' will be installed in the ticket hall.

Saint-Germain des Prés (line 4). This station serves a traditional literary area and the station will create a literary review for the passenger, with text extracts being projected onto the station vault, which will be changed every two weeks. The RATP anticipate that the public will be able to discover over 3,000 books per year.

Villejuif – Léo Lagrange (line 7). The theme at this 1985-built station will be sport, concentrating on famous people on the sports field. Floors will have marks related to athletic race tracks, rubbish bins will be akin to basketball hoops and seats will suggest Olympic rings in both form and colour. The station lighting will be likened to a sports stadium. There will also be a VDU featuring sports information.

Bonne Nouvelle (lines 8 and 9). This station serves the Grands Boulevards and the legendary Grand Rex cinema. The theme will be based on the cinema with the station being turned into a 'studio'. Cameras and screens will transmit news and the stairways will be decorated in Hollywood style with chrome ramps and relevant lighting.

Montparnasse – Bienvenüe (lines 4, 6 12 and 13). A small display on one of the line 6 platforms has already been devoted to Fulgence Bienvenüe, the 'father' of the Métro, but in this Millennium renovation the theme will be extended throughout the four-line complex. The ticket office area will commemorate the person himself, while platform posters will carry pictures highlighting technical progress during the Métro's 100-year existence. Corridor ceilings will be painted with pictures of RATP staff with passenger silhouettes projected onto them, bringing to life the interplay of passengers and staff.

Pasteur (lines 6 and 12). This station has already had small displays of science and medicine but the new work will promote the ideas of good health and well-being in daily life. Platform display panels will illustrate the evolution of ideas of health, the prevention of disease, diagnosis and hygiene. The station corridors will become 'labyrinths of feeling' with sight, hearing and touch being activated in turn by sounds of waterfalls, the seas and plays of light.

Europe (line 3). As the name of the station probably suggests, the theme will be the history and everyday life from member nations of the European Union. A different country will be highlighted each week.

Carrefour-Pleyel (line 13). This station will be transformed into an instrument of contemporary music, with a play on sound and light. The noises of the Métro will themselves be used and orchestrated into music for the passenger and will be linked to the passage of a train.

Station Entrances

It would be wrong to consider the stations of the Métro solely in terms of their interior design and to neglect one of their most characteristic features, the entrances. While the access stairways and passageways, constructed with due regard for economy, were undistinguished and, in many cases, very soon inadequate for the volume of traffic, the CMP, with some prompting from Charles Garnier, decide to make the entrances 'an object of beauty' and to this end organised a competition for their design. As far back as 1886, when it seemed likely that the long-discussed underground railway was about to be built, Garnier, the architect of the Paris Opéra, wrote to the then Minister of Public Works and urged that the Métro should shun all association with industry and turn instead to bronze and stone, marble and triumphal columns, adorned with sculptures. Nothing came of the 1886 project and the art form most closely associated with the Métro was one totally different from Garnier's classicism. None of the designs submitted – all very dependent on traditional ideas – pleased the Directors of the CMP and their final choice was rejected by the municipality. The Chairman of the company, banker Adrien Bernard, who was himself a great admirer of Art Nouveau, then had the inspired idea of awarding the commission to a relatively unknown young architect, Hector Guimard, who was only 32 at the time. Having qualified as an architect and won a travel scholarship, he did not follow the well trodden path to Rome, but instead went off to Brussels, where he studied under Vincent Horta, one of the first European exponents of Art Nouveau. Working in forged iron, Guimard created balustrades in which curves and hollows flowed into each other without beginning or end and the letter 'M' was created by their meeting. The entrances were marked by two curving uprights, at the end of which were flower like globes, illuminated at night. Between these was a plate with the name 'Métropolitain' in flowing letters and the signature of the architect. At the more important stations, the entrances were covered by pavilions in the same general style, but with variations. Bastille and Étoile were the only two to get station buildings almost monumental, with a touch of the oriental.

A station entrance designed by Guimard at Porte d'Auteuil, in the snow on 6 January 1995.
Julian Pepinster

Guimard was not without his critics, and as early as 1904 the CMP was persuaded to abandon the designs he had prepared for Opéra and to substitute rather pedestrian stone balustrades designed by Cassien Bernard. Nevertheless, some 87 Guimard entrances survive on lines 1 to 8, and in 1978 were given the protection of 'listed building' status.

Two have found their way into museums of modern art, in New York and Paris. The pavilions have fared less well and only Porte Dauphine on line 2 survives, blending quietly into the trees of the Avenue Foch. None of the canopies remain on their original site, but that from Hôtel de Ville was re-erected at Abbesses when displayed by the entry to an underground car park. While it adds character to the pretty little Montmartre square in which it stands, it is historically quite out of place, as the Nord-Sud at no time availed itself of Guimard's talents.

Apart from the stone balustrades mentioned above, Guimard's style gave way to a much more sombre design in wrought iron, designed by Dervaux. First used on the southern section of line 4, these entrances were generally used for all stations to be opened between the wars. They are marked by a column surmounted by a globe, illuminated at night. The Nord-Sud used a similar design, but with a more intricate design of balustrade. Reinforced concrete pavilions appeared on the extensions of the 1930s, generally used to provide covers for escalators.

Entrances constructed in recent years have used modern materials such as fibre-glass and are generally much lighter and simpler than those of earlier days. Present-day escalators can be unprotected and many exit directly onto the street. A post with a yellow 'M' is a rather plain successor to the Guimard entrances, although new totems have been designed for fitting to all line 14 station entrances in the near future.

The RATP were also out photographing in the snow on 6 January 1995. This photograph of a station entrance at Château de Vincennes on line 1 shows the less ornate railings surrounding the stairway and the globe lighting, typical of Métro entrances constructed from the 1920s. *RATP*

Other Station Services

Station ticket offices were originally very simple and not particularly inviting. Gradually, however, these have become more welcoming and where space permitted, other facilities such as news-stands, telephones, information booths and boutiques have been added to make available to passengers a wide range of services.

Within stations, directions are given with reference to the termini of a line – the visitor should memorise the names of the terminal stations! Intermediate stations are normally listed in the corridor or at the stairs giving access to a platform. These show the stations in line order, with interchanges on the right. On the platforms, exit signs are in blue and 'correspondance' (interchange) indications, leading to other lines are usually orange.

If there is more than one exit, plaques on the wall helpfully indicate the names of the streets and the house numbers to which each gives access. Ticket halls and some platforms have a very useful 'Plan du Quartier' which shows the streets and the more important buildings in the area, and exactly where the station entrances are situated. As an experiment the first television screens on the Métro appeared on the 23 December 1985 and by the end of December the following year 26 station platforms had the new facility. A total of 49 station platforms were ultimately equipped, relaying news, information and commercial advertising, the TV screens being either on pedestals or suspended from the ceilings. Known as 'Tube' the scheme did not attract advertisers and therefore did not meet its costs. The service terminated on 22 December 1989 and the screens were removed over the following two months.

Lifts

Although the original agreement of 1898 specified that the CMP should install lifts where there was a difference of 12 metres or more between street and platform level, or between the platforms of two corresponding lines, the CMP at first regarded lifts as an expense to be avoided, and the first was not placed in service (at République) until November 1910. Several more lifts were provided for the deeper stations on lines 4 and 7, but at the outbreak of the war in 1914, only seven stations were so equipped. Several more were placed in service when line 10 was opened and the Nord-Sud company could not avoid the provision of lifts at the deeper stations on line 12. However, they have always been relatively uncommon on the Métro and some of the earlier installations have now been replaced by escalators.

The first lifts were hydraulic, but those for lines 4 and 7 were electrically-powered. An unsuccessful return to hydraulic power was made with the lifts for line 10 and these were replaced by escalators. The first automatic lifts were placed in service at Havre – Caumartin on line 9 in 1937 and after 1945 all older lifts were gradually replaced by new ones for this method of operation. The general rate of travel is 3.5m/second.

As at 1 January 1999 there were 45 lifts at 17 stations, the deepest being at Buttes-Chaumont on line 7bis (28.70m). At certain stations, such as Saint-Michel and Cité on line 4, the lifts take passengers directly to and from platform level. A total of 20 lifts were provided for stage I of Météor line 14, to make this new Métro line accessible to all. Other stations undergoing a major rebuild will be similarly treated.

Escalators

While the average depth of Métro stations is not so great in comparison with those on London's tube lines, the development of escalators on the system was for many years a very slow process. Nevertheless, since the first practical escalator in the world was used at the Paris Exhibition in 1900, it is perhaps not surprising that escalators first appeared on the Métro before lifts did. The first escalator was installed at Père Lachaise in 1909, but even by 1923 only eight machines were in service. These early escalators were rather slow (65 steps/minute) and all were of the shunt landing type with passengers having to step off sideways on leaving. They were thus awkward to use, especially for ladies in fashionable tight hobble-skirts.

Escalators of the modern comb type with wooden-cleated treads had a speed of 90 steps/minute and were first used at Porte des Lilas in 1924. Again, development was slow and as late as 1966 there were only 87 in service at 50 stations. In general, escalators were installed only where the difference in height was over 4m and even then very often in the ascending direction only. In part, the use of escalators was held back by the automatic (portillon) gates, which closed off the platforms as trains arrived. As these very quickly led to the build up of a crowd (when closed), escalators could only be used where there was enough space for this crowd to form without blocking off would-be travellers.

As with the control of tickets, it was the coming of the RER which altered matters considerably. A programme drawn up in 1966 provided for the purchase of 200 new escalators, of which 34 were for the Métro. Since then, the growth in the number of escalators has been phenomenal, with 474 in use at 202 stations at 1 January 1999, which excludes a further 304 in operation on the RATP's RER network. This development has been helped by the introduction in 1973 of 'compact' escalators with a width overall of only 0.6m (as against a normal 1.0m) and an angle of incline 35° as opposed to the usual 30°. These do not require to be protected from the weather and at many places, such as bus interchange stations, they lead directly into the open. The first of the weatherproof escalators was commissioned at Place Monge on line 7. Density of passenger flow rather than depth of a station is now the main factor governing the installation of new escalators. It should be noted that some escalators on the Métro are controlled by photo-electric cells, and are set in motion by the approach of a passenger. If no others come along, the escalator stops again after sufficient time has elapsed for that passenger to have reached the top or bottom. The general speed of escalators on the Métro is now 100 steps/minute. The escalators with the greatest rise are at Places des Fêtes on line 7bis (22.45m), while the shortest are at Havre – Caumartin on line 3 (2.60m). A total of 97 Métro escalators have a rise less than 4m.

The following list of lines and numbers of escalators (a total of 474 at 202 stations) is as at 1 January 1999. Following a re-organisation of assets on a 'line' basis, all escalators at a station are allocated to one line only.

Line	Escalators	Stations	Line	Escalators	Stations
Line 1	33	13	Line 7bis	6	3
Line 2	13	6	Line 8	37	21
Line 3	41	15	Line 9	37	22
Line 3bis	4	1	Line 10	13	7
Line 4	89	22	Line 11	21	10
Line 5	16	9	Line 12	22	16
Line 6	25	10	Line 13	45	19
Line 7	40	23	Line 14	32	5

The early escalators installed on the Métro were quite similar to those on the London Underground, being manufactured by Otis and having wooden cleated steps. Although a few remain, most have now been replaced, but have given excellent service since the 1930s. *Brian Hardy*

Along with the station modernisation undertaken at Saint-Ambroise on line 9 in 1997, a new escalator was also installed. Manufactured by CNIM, it was then only one of two to have glass sides, the other being on RER line A at Bussy – Saint-Georges. *Brian Hardy*

Three levels at Madeleine connected by glass-sided escalators – ticket office level, line 12 level and line 14 below. All the escalators on line 14 (Météor) have glass sides. *Capital Transport*

Moving Walkways

Despite the initial planning of the Métro system, it was not always possible to ensure that the distances at interchange stations were as short as the public might have wished, and some of the corridors on the Métro are exceptionally long. The CMP had considered the idea of moving walkways in the 1930s but had been unable to put the idea into practice beyond ensuring that the necessary width was left in some passageways of new construction. It was not until 21 October 1964 that the first pair of moving walkways was put into service at Châtelet, linking lines 1 and 4 with 7 and 11. They were 131m long and 092m wide and had a speed of 45m/minute (2.7km/h) which allowed them to carry 10,000 passengers per hour. In service they proved to be slightly too small and slow, and when the next set (of three) was installed at Montparnasse Bienvenüe on 25 July 1968, they were made rather wider (1.12m) and had a speed of 3km/h, allowing a capacity of 11,000 passengers per hour. Two have also been installed at Invalides, connecting the Métro with RER line C. The total number of moving walkways on the Métro is thus seven, at three stations.

In 1942 the two close-by but separate stations of Montparnasse (lines 6 and 13) and Bienvenüe (lines 4 and 12) became one, Montparnasse Bienvenüe, but it was not until July 1968 that three moving walkways were installed, to reduce the interchange time through very long corridors of this combined station. This is on 10 March 1991 – after the Métro had closed for the night.
Julian Pepinster

Station names

When Baron Haussmann, Préfet de la Seine, drove 85 miles of new streets across Paris between 1855 and 1870, he obliterated many of the ancient villages, so that when the first line of the Métro opened in July 1900, there were few old villages to use for station names. Instead, the names of important buildings on the line of route were used, as well as the name of a Square (Place) or a street (Rue), mostly at right-angles to the line. It seems that some of the names had the 'Place de' and 'Rue de' prefixes dropped before the signs were installed at stations, apart from a few odd exceptions, which still survive (e.g. Place de Clichy, which avoids confusion with Porte de Clichy). With Métro stations spaced close together, names used had to be those of streets where the stations actually were. But as the system grew, the name of a street at right-angles to the first line could be parallel to the second line, for which it was clearly imprecise. In many cases, therefore, a second name was added for the interchange, but in others an entirely new name was used. At the ends of the lines, at the City boundaries, the prefix Porte (Gate) was used on station names, and remains the case today even though the City fortifications had been dismantled by 1920.

Considering France's history, generals and battles of the Napoleons are well represented in station names. There are 18 generals and five battles associated with Napoleon I, five generals and four battles associated with Napoleon III and seven generals and nine battles for the rest of French history. Such examples are at Cambronne (line 6), Daumesnil (6/8), Duroc (12/13), Kléber (6), Mouton-Duvernet (4) and Pelleport (3bis) – all generals and, Austerlitz (line 5), Pyramides (7), Iéna (9) and Wagram (3) – all battles of Napoleon I.

Double-barrelled names are not always of two streets at right-angles. There are innumerable combinations, but apart from double names in their own right, such as Buttes Chaumont or Chardon-Lagache, these can be what is in effect one street at right-angles but which changes its name as it crosses the line, or a street name combined with a square or bridge combined with a district, or two villages. As there is a flat fare on the Métro, and thus there is no need to ask for specific destination names when purchasing a ticket, passengers do not have to quote some very long names – e.g. 'Boulogne – Pont de Saint Cloud (Rhin et Danube)' on line 10, or 'Bobigny – Pablo Picasso (Préfecture – Hôtel du Département)' on line 5!

Name changes have, of course, taken place for various reasons. Apart from new lines which have caused name changes to interchange stations, the two world wars have also had their effects on Métro station names. For example, Berlin (Nord-Sud line B, now line 13) was closed in 1914 and later reopened as Liège. In the same year, Allemagne was swiftly renamed Jaurès, after a Socialist politician who had been assassinated in that year. During the First World War, Pont d'Austerlitz became Quai de la Rapée in 1916, and after that war Alma was renamed George V. Even though he was an Alsacian poet, Wilhem was renamed Église d'Auteuil in 1921, because the old name sounded too much like that of the German Kaiser!

After the Second World War, Franklin D. Roosevelt gave his name to a station in 1946 (previous name Marbeuf – Rond Point des Champs-Élysées), and seven stations were renamed after heroes of the resistance, including the two Corentins (Celton and Cariou) and Colonel Fabien (previously Combat). Corentin Celton was previously named Petits Menages and Corentin Cariou was Pont de Flandre.

In 1942 there were three big changes to give double-barrelled names to stations which had been hitherto linked as interchanges, but under separate names. Montparnasse (line 4 and 12) and Bienvenüe (lines 6 and 14) became Montparnasse – Bienvenüe, which still survives, but the other two have been changed again to become Franklin D. Roosevelt and Stalingrad, both in 1946.

Some names have disappeared from the map, only to re-appear elsewhere at a later date. These include Rue Saint-Denis which became Réaumur – Sébastopol in 1907, the first year of any name changes on the Métro, but was used in Boulevard Saint-Denis opened on line 4 in 1908, and by line 13 reaching the actual town of Saint-Denis in

1976. Austerlitz, disappearing in 1916, re-appeared as Gare d'Orléans – Austerlitz in 1930. Today, it is just plain Gare d'Austerlitz, even though the destinations of some trains on line 10 still refer to the previous name, from which it was renamed in 1977. Already mentioned is that Alma became George V in 1920, but Alma – Marceau opened in 1923. Torcy became Marx Dormoy in 1946, but re-appeared as a New Town at the end of the new branch on RER line A in 1980. Line 4's station at Vaugirard was renamed Saint-Placide in 1913, three years after the Nord-Sud company's Vaugirard station with the same name was opened – and remains so named to this day. In addition, the name Sèvres appears twice on the Métro – in Pont de Sèvres (line 9) and Sèvres-Babylone (lines 10 and 12).

In addition to all the main station names, there are many which have suffixes in their own right. For example Javel – André Citroën (the latter named after a 'quai' honouring the famous car manufacturer) and Porte d'Orléans – Général Leclerc, the suffix honouring the famous Free French General, who entered Paris at the head of his armoured division, and liberated Strasbourg. He was posthumously promoted 'Marshal' in 1952, so that the street and station names are technically incorrect. Another World War II hero is honoured in Porte Dauphine – Maréchal de Lattre de Tassigny.

Since 1970 there have been 13 alterations to station names on the Métro, some of them only in the form of suffixes added. Summarised, these are:

Year	Line(s)	Old Name	New Name
1970	2	Rue de Bagnolet	ALEXANDRE DUMAS
1970	1–2–6	Étoile	CHARLES DE GAULLE – ÉTOILE
1986	9	Nation	NATION – PLACE DES ANTILLES
1989	1–7	Palais Royal	PALAIS ROYAL – MUSÉE DU LOUVRE
1989	1	Louvre	LOUVRE – RIVOLI
1989	12	Chambre des Députés	ASSEMBLÉE NATIONALE
1989	5	Porte de Pantin	PORTE DE PANTIN – PARC DE LA VILLETTE
1989	7	Porte de la Villette	PORTE DE LA VILLETTE – CITÉ DES SCIENCES ET DE L'INDUSTRIE
1989	7–9	Chaussée d'Antin	CHAUSSÉE D'ANTIN – LA FAYETTE
1989	7	Pont Neuf	PONT NEUF – LA MONNAIE
1996	8	Maisons-Alfort – École Vétérinaire	ÉCOLE VÉTÉRINAIRE DE MAISONS–ALFORT
1998	8–9	Rue Montmartre	GRANDS BOULEVARDS
1998	13	Saint-Denis – Porte de Paris	SAINT-DENIS – PORTE DE PARIS – STADE DE FRANCE

Anomalies exist where station names differ on platforms from those shown on the diagrams inside trains. Grande Arche de La Défense assumed that name when line 1 was extended there in 1992 but is now shown in trains as La Défense – Grande Arche. With the opening of Saint-Denis – Université as the new terminus on line 13 in 1998, the previous terminal station of Saint-Denis – Basilique (Hôtel de Ville) became Basilique de Saint-Denis on the car line diagrams. Both versions, however, retain the '(Hôtel de Ville)' suffix.

Further station name changes are anticipated in the near future. On line 9, Rue des Boulets – Rue de Montreuil may become Rue des Boulets, and on line 3 Saint-Maur may become Rue Saint-Maur. Some additional suffixes are also expected to appear.

CHAPTER 5

Rolling Stock

The original rolling stock of the CMP had a distinct affinity with contemporary tramcars. The wooden-bodied cars were about 8m long and carried at most 50 passengers. They rode on four-wheeled trucks and had two 125hp motors. Air brakes were used. They were very heavy for their size, the motors weighing 18.5 tonnes and the trailers 8.5 tonnes. Two single-width sliding doors were provided on each side, one for entry and one for exit. Within a short time these were seen to be inadequate and after 1902 new deliveries had double width doors, the earlier cars being similarly converted. A total of 12 of the original motor cars were double ended, but the remainder had one driving cab.

The first trains on line 1 consisted of a motor coach pulling two trailers but very soon, this formation became insufficient to cope with the increasing traffic and in 1901 it was decided to strengthen these and to operate trains of seven or eight coaches on line 2. With multiple unit traction still in its infancy, there was no certainty that it would be able to cope with the demands of everyday Métro traffic and it was decided to adopt the Thomson 'double traction' system which had been devised in 1898 and was simple and robust, although it was somewhat limited in its ultimate potential. Current collection and control was by the leading motor coach and current was passed through a huge controller to the motors of both the leading and other motor coach at line voltage by a bus line. Where lines did not have a terminal loop, the second motor car was located at the rear and the bus line ran the whole length of the train. (It should be pointed out that while all the original lines built up to 1910 had terminal loops, very few of the temporary termini were provided with them). The motor coaches were often seen to be struggling on the ramps leading to the elevated section of line 2 but the double traction system had solved the capacity problem and an order for 284 vehicles was placed in 1903. However, the events of 10 August 1903 altered the way in which rolling stock technology was to develop, not only in Paris but in other countries' systems as well. Towards the end of the evening peak on 10 August 1903, a short circuit caused a fire to break out in the leading motor coach of a double traction train at Boulevard Barbès station (now Barbès – Rochechouart). The staff decided to use the following four coach train to push out the defective one to the siding at Belleville, both trains being emptied of then exasperated passengers. The convoy set off, despite there being large clouds of black smoke issuing from the disabled motor. Unfortunately the points at Belleville had not been set for the siding so it was decided to press on to the terminus at Nation. By now, the train was in tunnel and when it reached Ménilmontant a fire broke out with terrible strength. At that point, the following very crowded train had stopped at Couronnes, the preceding station, and the Station Master, with great promptitude, asked the passengers to leave the train, which was not only carrying its own passengers, but those from the two trains in front. The majority, however, stayed put until the cloud of smoke issued from the tunnel mouth and all the lights went out. Loss of life was considerable – 84 passengers perished in this disaster, killed by carbon monoxide.

There were many factors contributing to the disaster, but the immediate blame was put on the under-powered wooden motor coaches, and the order just placed was cancelled. As a temporary measure, the maximum train length was reduced to seven coaches with the two motor cars placed together at the head, but as soon as practicable they were withdrawn for conversion to bogie stock, the last running on 14 May 1906. The trailers were in some cases rebuilt as bogie motor coaches but others survived unaltered on lines 2, 5 and 6 until they were withdrawn between 1930 and 1932.

Two four-wheeled wooden-bodied cars have been reconstructed to original condition and are now on display at the RATPs headquarters building in Rue de Bercy. The motor car (MM1) has single siding doors while the trailer (B161) has a pair of double doors. They are seen being transferred to their new home on 24 January 1995, crossing the River Seine at Châtelet. *G. Potier*

The Pre-Classic Bogie Stock

The history of the Classic, Sprague Stock, is extremely complicated and because it is almost extinct, no more than a brief summary will be attempted here.

The first two prototype bogie motor coaches were delivered in December 1902 and April 1903. They had wooden bodies but the driving compartments and switchgear were encased in metal. They worked as double-traction units and spent all of their lives on line 2. In 1914–15 they were re-equipped with four motors but the experiment was unsuccessful and they were re-converted to two motor condition. These two vehicles, however, set the general standard of appearance for all Métro stock built up to 1937.

Even before the Couronnes fire, the CMP seem to have been considering the use of multiple-unit control, probably recognising that the double-traction equipment could only be a stop-gap. An eight-coach train with three two-axle motor coaches working in multiple was trialled on line 1 in November 1903 – so anxious were the CMP to see how it would perform, that it operated before official permission to use it was

The Sprague stock survived on line 3bis until July 1981 and operated in four-car formations which included a composite trailer. One such train is seen just before withdrawal at Gambetta, which used to be the through platform to central Paris on line 3 before it became a branch line in 1971.
John Herting

granted! This train used the Sprague system, which was then one of three then available. But wisely, the CMP spent much time and money evaluating the various systems both single and in combination before deciding in 1908 on the Sprague-Thomson system. It was an excellent choice and was to give 75 years of reliable service, standing up uncomplainingly to the overcrowded conditions and minimal maintenance of the Second World War. With this system, a small master controller energised one or more of a small number of train wires commanding self-contained automatic electro-magnetic contactor equipment. This gave easy and smooth control of acceleration and also allowed the grouping of motors so that one failure did not incapacitate the whole train. Following experiments, the first trains so equipped were placed in service in 1908 and from then to the 1930s, the Sprague-Thomson system gradually replaced all other forms of control and gave the CMP a secure and reliable fleet, with a high degree of standardisation not enjoyed by any other operator before or since. The only exception to this was a batch of 21 motor coaches with Jeumont-Heidmann equipment delivered in 1930 especially for the gradients encountered on line 3. However, although giving excellent results they could not be worked with Sprague-Thomson trains – the interests of standardisation thus prevailed and no more were purchased for the Métro.

As with the trials of equipment, the vehicle layouts changed with time. The two prototype motor coaches of 1902–03 were 11.15m long with two sets of double doors, but the first production cars of 1904–05, the 300 class, were 10.85m long. In 1905, 114 rebuilds of four-wheel motor cars were placed in service and were identical in appearance to the 300 class, which was followed by a further batch of 56 two-axle rebuilds in 1906–07. A second group of cars, the 400 class, were built in 1904–05 and were 13.35m long, having had three sets of double doors. The 300 class motor cars were rebuilt in 1910 to make them identical with the 400 class and both classes received four motors in 1929–32, surviving unchanged until withdrawn from the late-1960s.

The Classic Stock

The next batch of new coaches, the 500 class, continued with the longer length of the 400 class. They had all-metal bodywork and were introduced from 1908. They were the first to have the Sprague-Thomson equipment and may thus be regarded as the definitive version of the Classic Stock. Their history was much less complicated than other groups and the class survived intact until the late-1960s. They were followed in 1909 by the broadly similar 600 class and in 1913–14 by the 700 class.

The motor coaches delivered after the First World War were characterised by a much smaller switchgear compartment (with the equipment being located under the car body) and with the consequent enlargement of the passenger accommodation – car length was increased to 13.60m. This series appeared between 1921 and 1927 and 18 of them were double-ended for use on line 10 and the Porte des Lilas – Pré-Saint-Gervais shuttle.

To improve service speeds on busier lines it was decided in 1925 to introduce four-motored motor cars (M4), and increase vehicle length to 14.20m. The first batch of 62 cars went into service in 1927–28 but retained three double doors per side – subsequent batches had four pairs of double doors. About half were built new while the rest were rebuilds of earlier Pre-Classic stock. The four-motor stock could always be distinguished by a small observation window to the right of the driving cab. The last batches of four-motor cars had the arrangement of the doors and windows equally spaced on each side.

The Nord-Sud motor coaches did not differ greatly from their contemporaries on the CMP and although built over the period 1909–25, and apart from their painted or enamelled exterior finish, were all visually identical to each other. They were slightly larger in profile and heavier than the CMP stock and had a much improved design of bogie. As they had less powerful motors, their progress was comfortable and stately rather than lively! The Nord-Sud company chose a different current collection system from that of the CMP. To avoid the problem of voltage drop without building many substations, the Nord-Sud was electrified on a three-wire 1,200V system. The leading motor picked up current at +600V from an overhead wire via a small pantograph, and the rear motor coach took current at –600V from a third rail. In an emergency, however, both could operate from either pickup at 600V only. Apart from one coach scrapped as a result of an accident just after the Nord-Sud merged with the CMP, all were incorporated into CMP stock in 1930. At this time, the overhead current system was abandoned in favour of the CMP standard 3rd rail system.

One coach was damaged by bombing in 1944 and, with eight others, was rebuilt for works train duties in 1952. All the others, however, survived in service until 1971–72, when the change in line voltage from 600 to 750V d.c. resulted in their sudden demise.

The first bogie trailers were delivered with the 400 class motors, which they closely resembled, although the first class vehicles were panelled in metal and were thus the first coaches to be painted rather than varnished. Many more trailers followed in the period 1908–13 and were based on the 500 class motor cars. The first trailers 13.60m long appeared from 1923, which were followed by four-door trailers 14.20m long, corresponding to the four-motored motor coaches. The Nord-Sud trailers closely resembled that system's motor cars but were fitted with rectangular windows in the car ends.

The original livery of the Classic Stock was varnished wood and when the first all-metal Classic Stock coaches appeared, they were painted dark brown to match. Later this was changed to a dark painted ('olive') green. From 1913 new stock was delivered with a medium green enamelled finish, while from 1930 all new M4 stock was delivered with a much brighter green enamelled finish. The new trains on line 1, introduced in the mid-1930s, were in what was officially called a grey-blue livery, but because of fading, the 'blue' was left to the imagination. First class trailers of the CMP were at first denoted by two white boards with '1st class' written on them, carried below the waist rail but when the green livery was adopted for second class, first class trailers became red. The Nord-Sud, ever different, used pleasing shades of royal and light blue/grey on their trains, with first class trailers being cream (almost light yellow) with red ends.

The grey Sprague trains operated exclusively on line 1 until their replacement by rubber tyred trains in 1963-64, when they moved to other lines, replacing older Sprague trains. M433 is at the rear of a train on line 2 departing Stalingrad on 12 May 1980. *Brian Hardy*

The interiors of all varieties of the Classic Stock was simple to the point of austerity. The seats in second class were of varnished wood, while the first class boasted leather upholstery but without a great deal of padding! Lighting was by three strips of 5×40w bulbs and ventilation was provided by pull-down windows (on one side of the coach only to prevent cross draughts) and by wide open vents in the lantern roof. Neither heating or sound insulation was provided and the train noises were thus most enjoyable for the enthusiast, particularly in the motor cars and especially in the seats behind the driver!

The driving cabs were simply equipped, the driver sitting (but more often standing) on the right, working the master controller with his right hand and the air brake valve with his left. The only instrument provided was the air-brake pressure gauge and the speed was left to the driver's judgement. Glazed doors and panels gave the passengers a good view of all this as well as the 'fireworks' from the traction line switches which were mounted, often without any covering, on the left-hand side of the cab. There was no deadman's handle but the master controller sprang back to the 'off' position if released and could not be moved away from that position unless the button in the centre of the handle was first depressed. Furthermore, the guard travelled in the leading coach and operated from the leading pair of doors and was thus in sight of the driver.

In summary, there were numerous batches of Sprague stock, each one representing a small piece of a very large jigsaw puzzle for ultimate service requirements. Many different car builders were involved over the years which, at its maximum in 1937, amounted to 2,720 cars, summarised as follows:

Driving Motor Cars ('M')	CMP M4 (Rebuilds)	340	
	CMP M4 (new cars)	257	
	CMP M2	626	
	NS M4	114	1337
First Class Trailers ('Ab')	CMP	348	
	NS	51	399
Second Class Trailers ('Bb')	CMP	682	
	NS	100	782
Composite Trailers ('AB')	CMP	202	202
			2720

The interior of the Sprague stock was basic, to say the least. Comfort was in the form of wooden slatted seats and ventilation was through open lantern roofs — there were no heaters. This is a typical interior with the enamel panelling with the original company's 'CMP' monogram.
John Herting

By 1937 the CMP had at its disposal a highly standardised fleet of trains with simple and rugged equipment which was a godsend during the difficult war years, when maintenance was at a minimum and traffic was at maximum breaking point. These virtues however, became a drawback in the early post-war period, for although the newest cars were but a few years old, their design dated back to 1903! The Métro was regarded as noisy and antiquated. A number of experiments were made with fluorescent lighting and regenerative braking, for example, but these were intended to try out new ideas for the next generation of rolling stock rather than to improve the Classic Stock.

Apart from two cars that were destroyed in the Second World War, systematic withdrawal of the Classic Stock began only with the conversion of line 1 to 'pneu' operation in the early 1960s. Even then, many trains were transferred to reinforce other lines, rather than being sent to the scrap yard, while other (motor) cars were converted into works motor cars. It was only when the MF67 stock began to arrive that serious inroads were made in the ranks of the Sprague trains, which disappeared from lines 3 and 7 in 1971 and 1973 respectively, although some of them went to line 12 to replace the Nord-Sud stock. The extensions of line 8 into the suburbs in the early 1970s created a need for more trains and this gave the Sprague stock a chance to show its paces on the new Créteil section, where the stations are more widely spaced than in central Paris. During the 1970s, Sprague stock gave way to 'pneu' trains on line 6 in 1974 and to the articulated stock on line 10 (1975–76), while the last of the two-motored motor coaches went from line 2 (being replaced by four-motored coaches) in 1976. With the arrival of the MF77 stock, and by the 'cascade' transfer of other modern stock between various lines, Sprague stock disappeared from lines 5, 7bis, 8 and 12 in 1980 and lines 2 and 3bis in 1981. In the following year, just 16 trains remained at work on line 9 and these would have gone by September if it had not been for a severe flood at Église de Pantin on line 5 on 6 June 1982, which severely damaged 18 trains of MF67 stock which had to be rebuilt electrically. This gave a stay of execution and the last Sprague trains were finally withdrawn in April 1983.

The Classic Stock not only set the visual aspect for some 79 years between 1904 and 1983, it also brought many unique sounds (from the electrical equipment) and smells (from the oiled-wood brake blocks), and the Métro no longer seems the same without it. It was an extraordinary and successful long career.

When the Métro's power supply was upgraded and the voltage increased from 600V to 750V, the Nord-Sud stock on line 12 had to be withdrawn. Five cars, however, were retained for preservation, one of them previously residing in the now closed Saint-Mandé Museum. At Mirabeau on line 10 on 23 September 1993 Ab1036 and M2103 pass through on a transfer trip from Auteuil to Invalides. *C. Prodanovic*

However, they did not simply fade away. The Parisians realised that part of their city's history was about to pass away. The RATP therefore commemorated the event with a ceremony never before (and since) accorded to an underground train. A series of planned events took place between 11 and 16 April 1983 under the title of 'Salut l'Artiste', which included displays and exhibitions and a train stabled in the bay platform at Concorde on line 8 selling transport souvenirs. Meanwhile, four Sprague trains (three of them decorated with special themes) ran to a published timetable on line 9 between the peaks to cater for those who wanted a last ride. The official RATP farewell took place on Friday afternoon 15 April, when three trains carried officially invited guests from Porte de Montreuil to Pont de Sèvres and into Boulogne depot. The last public runs took place the following day on Saturday 16 April 1983.

In fact, the last trains in April did not result in the Sprague stock to be 'gone and forgotten'. To the contrary in fact, and the first enthusiast tours after their withdrawal operated on various lines in January 1985. Since then, many trips with the surviving trains have operated both during the day and at night, but more recently, the operational trains have been confined to line 3bis (day time) or in non-traffic hours on other lines. With the Centenary of the Métro in July 2000, the operational Sprague sets are being thoroughly overhauled with additional safety modifications being made. This will enable them to work 'in traffic' on special occasions, and will give these operational museum pieces pride of place marking such a special event.

In addition, there are a number of other Sprague cars in store, and they include the museum pieces which resided in the Paris Transport Museum at Saint-Mandé and those remaining in RATP ownership.

Many other coaches of Sprague stock survive elsewhere, both in the French provinces and abroad. Perhaps pride of place must go to motor car M1354 which can be found in the Railway Museum at Mulhouse, and the rebuilt four-wheeled cars of 1900 and 1902 vintage which are on display in the reception area of the Maison de la RATP (the headquarters building of the RATP) in Rue de Bercy, adjacent to Gare de Lyon main line station.

Summary of wooden and Sprague stock – 1 February 1999

Train sets for special events and filming –
M1269 – Bb434 – Ab475 – Bb761 – M1350‡
M333 – Bb751 – Ab487 – Bb572 – M103
M429 – Bb782 – Ab411 – Bb713 – M1308   (Grey train)   } Not in use
M270 – M1266   Spare cars   }
Exhibition/Reception train, Porte Maillot disused station (arrival platform) –
M517† – Bb546 – Ab253 – Bb240 – M757†
Maison de La RATP, adjacent to Gare de Lyon main line station in Rue de Bercy –
MM1 – B161   (Rebuilt four-wheeled cars)
M857†
Ex-Transport Museum Saint-Mandé (closed), vehicles stored –
M305† – M535† – Ab167 – M102* – A1§
Mulhouse Museum –
M1354
Other RATP-owned vehicles –
M1079
M473 – M1231 – M1316 – M1322
M2103* – M2104*
Ab284 – Ab464 – Ab1036* – Ab1037*
Bb171 – Bb453
AB5338

Note   * Nord-Sud stock   ‡ Listed as 'National Heritage' on 18 December 1998
        † M2 motor coach   § Rebuilt 4-wheeled first class trailer

A small number of Tracteurs are allocated exclusively to 'pilot' duties, to transfer equipment and individual Métro cars between depots and workshops. On a transfer of equipment trip on 19 November 1998, TA02 is nearest the camera in the new service stock livery of yellow and maroon, reversing at Place Monge on line 7, before proceeding to line 10. *Brian Hardy*

Other Sprague stock survivors had less glamorous roles. Many have been converted to 'Tracteurs' (motor cars for engineering trains), the majority of post-war conversions being double-ended, two motor coaches (less their trailing ends) making one Tracteur. Early works motor cars included the double-ended wooden four-wheeled motors (MM1–12) displaced from passenger train duties in 1906 but surviving until 1949. Early conversions began in 1922 with T1 and T2 (ex-M313 and M316), followed by another 29 converted in the period 1928–37. The last conversions were undertaken in 1969–72. All are fitted with both conventional and 'pneu' system shoe-gear, to enable them to work over all lines. Similarly, many trailers have been converted over the years into wagons of various types, performing diverse roles, which bear the prefix 'V' or 'VX', while some ex-trailers retain their upper body work, being used as workshops for injection trains' staff. A total of 14 new battery locomotives (TMA), built by Alsthom, were delivered in 1985–86, enabling some engineers trains to work 'on current' or on battery power.

The rationalisation of the works train fleet is envisaged over the next few years. This includes the purchase of 14 new Tracteurs (TNG – Tracteur Nouvelle Génération). The new TNG locomotives will be similar in appearance to the existing TMAs but will be without battery power. The traction motors will be acquired from withdrawn MS61 stock from the RER. However, a small number of Sprague Tracteurs are expected to survive until 2006–07.

The following works train vehicles were available as at 31 March 1999:

Tracteurs 'T'	45	Non-bogie 2-axle wagons 'V'	6
Tracteurs Ateliers 'TA'	13	Plasser machine	1
Battery locomotives 'TMA'	14	PLC (Driving Trailer for TMA)	4
Bogie vehicles/wagons 'V'	127	TMVI (Slow-speed Tracteur	1
Tracteur Diesel	3	for Tunnel Cleaning Train)	
Matisa	1	Bogie wagons ('VX')	3

There is also a Rail Grinding train on semi-permanent loan from Speno SA, Italy.

The Articulated (MA51) Stock

After the end of the Second World War, studies were instituted for new rolling stock which, by virtue of improved acceleration and braking, would improve overall service speed and thus increase line capacity. These studies ultimately resulted in the articulated trains, the first of which arrived in September 1951 and went into service on Line 13 in February 1952. The impending extension of this line from Porte de Saint-Ouen to Carrefour Pleyel (opened on 30 June 1952) made an increase in line capacity imperative.

The car bodies were built by Brissoneau et Lotz and each semi-permanently coupled unit consisted of three car bodies resting on four bogies. The outer cars of a unit were 12.70m long and the middle car shorter, at 9.70m. The outer (driving) cars were second class only, while the middle car was a composite. The two articulated bogies per unit were motored, while the two outer bogies were trailer bogies. These trains introduced a new colour scheme of light blue and grey for second class and cream with blue lining for first class. Internally, the new stock represented a great step forward, having upholstered seating in both classes, fluorescent lighting and, improved ventilation. Each unit was equipped with four self-ventilated motors of 92hp controlled by type JH servo-motor-operated cam-contactor controllers. The bogies were of welded construction and incorporated 'Athermos' axle boxes with radial movement. Most of the bogies were constructed by Alsthom, but in three units by BL (E036, 039 and 040). On the articulated parts, rubber 'Silentblocs' were used. Braking was by Westinghouse air brakes and brake release is done electro-pneumatically under the control of a decelerometer, giving adequate retardation without wheel slip. The trains were fitted with Scharfenberg automatic couplers at the driving ends, but semi-permanently coupled within units.

Although given unit numbers, the articulated stock also had individual car numbers, driving cars prefixed 'D' and the shorter middle cars prefixed 'C' as follows:

Unit	Formation
E001	D01–C01–D02
E002	D03–C02–D04

and so on, up to

E040	D79–C40–D80

Being over 20 years old, a prototype refurbishment was undertaken at Vaugirard workshops from August 1974, being completed in March 1975, unit E030 being selected. The work involved utilising noise-reducing materials, increasing the fluorescent lighting, and installing tip-up seats at all door positions. The exteriors were repainted in a royal blue and white livery with a dark blue waist band, the first class section being denoted by a yellow band at cantrail height. The modernisation work on the other 39 units was undertaken at Saint-Ouen workshops, following deliveries of new MF67 stock to line 9, which reduced the amount of work to be done at that depot on the old Classic stock. The work on the MA51 stock was also to improve its reliability, and to give it a new lease of life. It was completed by the autumn of 1976 and allowed the replacement of the 1926–36 Sprague stock on line 10. At the same time, a small number of five car trains of MF67 stock were allocated to line 10, as the 20 trains of MA51 stock alone were insufficient to provide the complete service on that line.

In service, the MA51 stock did much of what was expected of it, especially with regard to acceleration, but it was noisy and rough riding and the design was not repeated. Original plans, however, proposed further builds and run them in three-unit formations on the busiest lines, whose platforms would have had to be lengthened to 105m. Nevertheless, these trains gave sound service for over 40 years, at first on line 13, and from 1975–76 on line 10, the latter incorporating the refurbishment.

With line 13 being a 'Y'-shaped line, the articulated MA51 stock was ideal for uncoupling and operating short (one-unit) trains in service at certain off peak times. However, uncoupling ceased in 1972, not only with the stock's imminent transfer to line 10, but also to eliminate the operating problems associated with uncoupling and the extra staff needed for it.

On the refurbished MA51 stock, the position of the first class accommodation was changed, as on line 10 the units would not be required to uncouple. The first class was thus moved to the standard position in the middle of the train. This was achieved by converting one driving car of half of the 40 units and ensuring that they were always formed in the middle of a train. The odd-numbered driving car of each odd-numbered unit was selected for first class accommodation and therefore each train comprised one odd and one even-numbered unit. With semi-permanent train formations, the middle driving cabs became redundant, only equipment needed for shunting being retained (and locked away out of use when in service, so that the area could be used by passengers). The traffic levels, and as a result, service intervals, on line 10 do not warrant the investment of Automatic Train Operation, and thus the MA51 stock always operated in conventional driving mode, but one-person-operated.

The first withdrawals of the MA51 stock occurred in July 1987 but it was to be a further seven years before the last runs were made in service. This occurred on 15 June 1994 and the farewell train comprised units E034+E023. The protracted withdrawal period was due in part, to the equally protracted delivery and entry into service of the MF88 trains on line 7bis, which ultimately enabled the transfer of some MF67E trains from that line to line 10. The few trains that survived at the end of 1993 acquired the new RATP logos, but retained their royal blue livery.

One car from unit E001 originally resided at the RATP's Technical School but has now been scrapped, while E010 has been retained by the RATP in non-operational condition. In addition, E023 is privately preserved by the ADEMAS group.

There were initially high hopes for the articulated MA51 stock, which originally went into service on line 13, with large orders expected for other busier lines. However, no more trains were ordered after the first batch of 40 units. They were transferred in refurbished condition to line 10 in 1975-76, where they stayed until withdrawn. Leading is driving car D25 of unit E013 at Mabillon, taken a few days before the stock was finally withdrawn. Those that survived at the end of 1993 did acquire the new RATP logo, although they did not receive the new house livery of green and white. *Julian Pepinster*

The RATP abandoned further orders of articulated stock and concentrated instead on new ideas. They came up with rubber tyres and an experimental car was constructed and tried on the shuttle line (Navette) between Porte des Lilas and Pré-Saint-Gervais. This was taken on 18 August 1954 and shows the single coach at the former. *RATP*

The 'Pneu' Stock

The need for greater line capacity than could be obtained with conventional stock, and the great expense of lengthening stations to allow longer trains to be operated, caused a novel alternative to be considered by the RATP. Greater line capacity was to be obtained with the aid of high acceleration and retardation given by the use of rubber tyres, and higher maximum speeds between closely spaced stations could be gained by the same means. Extra comfort and lightweight vehicles would also be obtained.

Plans were thus formulated for experiments with rubber-tyred train operation. The 767m-long 'shuttle' line between Porte des Lilas and Pré-Saint-Gervais was chosen, which had been closed to passengers since September 1939, and a special single car was built in 1951 by a consortium of manufacturers, with two 130hp Alsthom motors and Jeumont equipment. The motors were hung from the body, instead of being mounted on the bogies in the usual way, and drove the axles by cardan drive. A small pantograph, not normally visible, was fitted for shunting purposes. For the first time rheostatic braking was fitted, backed up by electro-pneumatic brakes, with automatic deceleration and braking for normal service. The coach was classified 'MP51' and carried the stock number of 151 at each end. It was delivered on 25 July 1951 and was made available for inspection by the press and public on 12 and 14 November 1951. The coach underwent exhaustive tests and trials and entered service on 13 April 1952 carrying passengers between 13.30 and 19.30 on the shuttle line. The trials included experiments with Automatic Train Operation. The car was withdrawn from service on 31 May 1956 and, being an experiment, the service was not replaced. The car was put into store in 1961 and in April 1981 was taken to the Paris Transport Museum at Saint Mandé where it was put on display to the public, representing a very important stage in the transition of Paris Métro rolling stock.

For rubber-tyred train operation, the track has to be specially converted. It consists of conventional steel rails, which are retained as 'safety' rails, flanked by longitudinal hardwood tracks (now replaced on the main lines), reinforced concrete, or wide metal 'I' beams. Vertical guide bars, which are also the conductor rails, are arranged 2.44m apart on insulating supports.

The bogies have rubber-tyred carrying wheels with tyres 1m in diameter, inflated to $9kg/cm^2$ (motor) or $6.5kg/cm^2$ (trailers). Inside there are conventional steel wheels with deep flanges which drop onto the safety rail if a tyre becomes deflated. Braking is by oiled-wood blocks onto these wheels. Shoes rubbing on the safety rails give both negative return and track circuit operation for automatic signalling. Spring loaded shoes press sideways onto the guide bars for current collection. Guide wheels on vertical axles fit between the guide bars – their tyres are 0.54m diameter, inflated to $9kg/cm^2$.

At points and crossings, the longitudinals are lowered to the level of the steel rails and the guide rails interrupted – the deep flanges of the steel wheels then guide the train. Severe speed limits are in force at these locations.

From these experiments it was decided that the idea of rubber-tyred train operation on the Métro was sound and the whole of line 11 was chosen for conversion to 'pneu' operation. Although a relatively short line, 6.287km from Châtelet to Marie des Lilas, it nevertheless had a wide variety of technical problems to offer, such as many curves and an almost continual gradient at 1 in 25. The new stock for line 11 was formed into four-car sets formed of two driving motors (M), one non-driving motor car (N) and one composite trailer (AB), in the formation M-N-AB-M. Known as the MP55 type, it was built in two separate batches, as follows:

Type

MP55A	M3001–3020		
MP55A	N4001–4010*	}	Bodies and bogies by RNUR
MP55A	AB55501–5510		equipment by CEM
MP55B	M3021–3036		Bodies by Brissonneau et Lotz
MP55B	N4011–4018*	}	bogies by Alsthom, equipment
MP55B	AB5511 5517		by Jeumont

Note *N4001–4018 were originally numbered N3501–3518 respectively. Renumbered in 1962.

The main difference between this stock and its predecessors lies, of course, with its bogies, but the opportunity was taken to introduce some modifications in design of the bodywork to improve the general standard of comfort offered to the travelling public. Despite being of two different batches, however, all were identical and operationally compatible.

The driving cars were 15m long, the non-driving cars and trailers 14.39m. To improve passenger flow, the width of the door openings was increased to 1.30m. The doors operated pneumatically and could be opened by simply raising a latch as the train comes to a halt. When closing, the rate of travel slows down as the doors come together, in marked contrast to the Sprague stock, whose doors met with a hefty 'clump', and in their day no doubt accounted for many a crushed (and sore) finger! Lighting and suspension were improved and, for the first time, sliding ventilators were fitted to the windows – on both sides of the car. Partly because of these, the noise level was reduced considerably. Internally, the cars were much like the articulated MA51 stock and they were painted in the same livery.

Each motor car had four 90hp axle-hung motors and JH-type cam-contactor controllers were fitted. Acceleration progresses under time control so that it was much the same whether the train was empty or full – the acceleration and deceleration rates of $1.3m/s^2$ (which could be increased to $2.5m/s^2$ in emergency), together with the excellent adhesion given by rubber tyres, gave these trains very good performance, even on the severe curves and gradients on line 11.

Work on converting the trackwork on line 11 commenced in 1954. The first car of MP55 stock (N3501) was presented to the public on the Avenue des Champs-Élysées on 27 July 1956, while the first train was delivered on 10 October 1956, entering service on 13 November 1956, following an official launch on 8 November. Other trains followed up to the October of 1957. A total of 17 four-car trains were able to be formed, leaving two driving motor cars and one non-driving motor car spare. These in fact did not enter service until required much later (3036 in February 1958, 3021 in April 1958 and 4018 in April 1961) and thus it will be appreciated that formations did not remain constant. This became more evident in later years when, from 1977, a programme of renovation began, to bring the MP55 cars up to the standard of the MP73 type (q.v. below). Work included increasing the fluorescent lighting and fitting outside door indicator lights. Ventilation was also improved by fitting directional vents. The renovation of the cars was done singly and because painting into royal blue and white livery was not necessarily done at the same time, trains could be seen in service in both liveries and in modified or unmodified form.

Following on from the experiments on the Navette, line 11 was converted to rubber tyred operation in its entirety and trains of MP55 stock began service in the autumn of 1956. In later years
some of these trains were painted in the later royal blue and white livery, as seen at Pyrénées.
Brian Hardy

Scrapping of the MP55 stock began in 1995, although two cars (3028 and 4014) had
been out of use since 1979. The process quickened during 1997–98 with the arrival of
the MP89 stock on line 1, which released refurbished trains of MP59 stock from line
1 to 4, and refurbished four-car trains of MP59 stock from line 4 to line 11 (q.v. below).
The last train of MP55 stock (M3001–N4009–AB5503–M3030) ran in service on line
11 on Saturday 30 January 1999, which was celebrated in the usual Parisian tradition
at such events – although not so grandiose as with the Sprague stock. Even towards
the end, the original livery survived, running in mixed livery formations with the later
royal blue colours. No cars of MP55 stock received the new RATP green/white livery,
however. Two cars, one by each manufacturer, have been retained by the RATP, being
M3011 and AB5517. M3001 has been acquired for preservation by the builder Renault,
while M3002 survives as a night club, and M3032 has passed into private ownership.

The last day of operation of the first generation of rubber tyred trains of MP55 stock was on 30
January 1999, after over 40 years of passenger service. Right to the end, a few cars retained their
original livery, as seen on the commemorative special at Place des Fêtes on the last day.
Julian Pepinster

Following the success of line 11's conversion to 'pneu' operation, the next line to be converted was line 1, then the Metro's busiest. In original livery, a train of MP59 stock rounds the curve at Bastille. *John Herting*

The line 11 'pneu' conversion was considered very much still an experiment, but its success prompted the RATP to begin a programme of conversion of all of its lines, starting with line 1, then line 4 the two busiest Métro lines. It took a considerable period of time, however, to convert the trackwork, and then another year or so to introduce the rolling stock – the complete line's trackwork had to be converted before even one 'pneu' train could operate. On line 1, track conversion began in 1960 and new rolling stock was introduced between 31 May 1963 and December 1964. The conversion of line 4 followed and the stock was phased in from 3 October 1966 until August 1967. The rolling stock for both lines 1 and 4 was of one type the MP59 – but was delivered in three batches of four groups, the last of which was not delivered until 1972/73 to supplement existing trains on those two lines for increased services. All MP59 trains were built by CIMT with ANF bogies and Jeumont equipment and were formed into six-car trains, comprising two driving motor cars (M), two non-driving motor cars (N), one composite trailer (AB) and one first class trailer (A): M-N-AB-A-N-M.

The stock was numbered as follows:

Type			
MP59A	M3037–3128	MP59C	M3159–3224
MP59A	N4019–4110	MP59C	N4141–4206
MP59A	AB5518–5563	MP59C	AB5577–5607
MP59A	A6001–6046	MP59C	A6060–6090
MP59B	M3129–3158	MP59D	M3225–3240
MP59B	N4111–4140	MP59D	N4207–4222
MP59B	AB5564–5576	MP59D	AB5608–5616
MP59B	A6047–6059	MP59D	A6091–6100

Interior of MP59 stock in original condition and before refurbishment. The gaps in the fluorescent lighting made these trains look rather drab inside compared with the lighting on refurbished and newer stocks. *Brian Hardy*

The most noticeable difference between the earlier 'pneu' trains (the MP55) on line 11 and the later ones of lines 1 and 4 (MP59) is the adoption of a wide single-span windscreen on the driving cabs of the latter trains. On these, the traction motors are rated at 140hp as against 90hp of the MP55 cars. One of the additional trains built in 1973 (3235–4217–6069–5613–4218–3236) was equipped with thyristor 'chopper' control, operating in service on line 1 until 1979, then on line 4. It was sub-classified MP59DK but was converted to MP59D standard in 1985.

The original six-car formations of the MP59 stock comprised one trailer car ('A') and one-third of the adjacent trailer ('AB') with first class accommodation. During 1981–83, all the composite ('AB') cars on line 1 and 4 were converted to second class, giving one car out of six available for first class passengers, (compared to one out of five cars on most other lines). This involved removing the partition 'wall' inside the cars, which separated the two classes. From 1 March 1982, first class travel on all lines was restricted to between the hours of 09.00 and 17.00 daily. Previously it had applied from 08.00 and then throughout each day until the end of service. Insofar as the MP59 'AB' trailers were concerned, all that needed to be done was to alter the interior and exterior '1' to '2' on the old livery cars and to remove the appropriate section of yellow band from the newer liveried cars. When first class on the Métro was abolished altogether from 1 August 1991, a similar operation followed on the relevant cars.

With the extension of line 1 to La Défense to operate a short distance in the open air over the River Seine west of Pont de Neuilly, the MP59 trains on line 1 would have to be modified for 'outdoor' working. Being some 25 years old, the opportunity was taken to refurbish the trains at the same time, the work being undertaken by the RATP at Fontenay workshops (seven trains), Cannes La Bocca Industries (22 trains) and Ateliers de Constructions du Centre, Clermont Ferrand (23 trains). The 45 trains not refurbished by the RATP were transferred by road. A prototype refurbishment was undertaken on M3125 in 1989, following which the programme commenced later in the year. The first two trains returned to enter service on line 1 on 7 March 1990, the programme being completed in September 1992. The car interiors were gutted and new safety materials and finishes used. New vandal proof seating was fitted and the roof ventilation was modified to take into account open air running. Additional fluorescent lighting has been fitted. The cab ends were redesigned at roof level and all-round beading was fitted on the cab front. A completely new livery (albeit short lived) was introduced, comprising white with blue passenger doors and a black front. This last feature has continued on all subsequent refurbished trains.

Cars of MP59 stock at Bastille, showing the pre-1982 situation when six-car trains had a car and one third of first class accommo-dation. This is in the original livery, when first class cars were painted cream.
John Herting

The 52 refurbished trains of MP59 stock on line 1 were not, however, destined to continue service on that line, for new MP89 stock was to replace them to enable their transfer to line 4. Unrefurbished MP59 trains on line 4 would be scrapped, save for a number required for transfer to line 11, which would first be refurbished. A total of 84 cars were refurbished from the MP59B/C groups, forming 20 four-car trains (M-N-A-M). There are also three spare motor cars, the fourth vehicle having to be scrapped because of fire damage before refurbishment. The work was split between Cannes La Bocca Industries (39 cars) and ACC at Clermont Ferrand (44 cars), the road transportation being arranged from Saint-Ouen workshops. The first two trains were completed in December 1994, the project being completed in May 1995. On return, most of the trains returned to service on line 4 and each were formed up with two unrefurbished cars. Ultimate transfer to line 11 was undertaken minus the two un-refurbished cars, although all operated in the new green/white livery, the unrefurbished cars comprising adhesive material over the original colours. With the transfer of MP59 six-car refurbished trains from line 1 to line 4, this has enabled the four-car refur-bished trains on line 4 to go to line 11 and the two unrefurbished cars from each set going for scrap. The unrefurbished six-car trains of MP59 stock will then be scrapped once the MP89 stock provides the service on line 1, which is at present half complete.

MP59 stock painted in the royal blue and white livery of the mid-1970s. First class was indicated by having a yellow band at roof level, as on main line stock.
John Herting

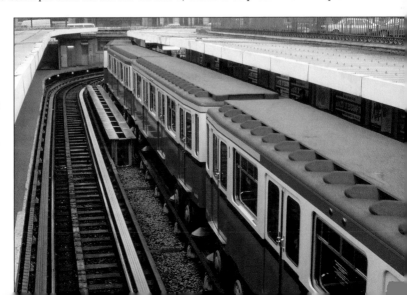

A bogie for rubber tyred trains, seen in Fontenay depot. Note the horizontal rubber guide wheels. Steel wheels are provided, and are used at points and crossings, and on the rare occasion that a tyre deflates. Because the steel wheels sit slightly above the running rail, they have deep flanges. *Brian Hardy*

Between 1989 and 1992, the 52 trains of MP59 stock on line 1 were refurbished, in readiness for the extension to La Défense, which contained a short section of open-air running. In refurbished condition, the trains were given a unique livery of white with blue doors, which turned out to be rather short-lived. The train front gives the appearance of being altered, but a little restyling at roof level is all that has taken place. Sporting the new RATP logo, a train arrives at Bastille. *Brian Hardy*

The introduction of the new corporate RATP livery of jade green and white saw the end of the white/blue livery on MP59 refurbished trains. The new finish is seen on this train rounding the corner into Bastille. *Brian Hardy*

For reasons that will become apparent in the next rolling stock section (MF67), the RATP decided to abandon its plan to convert all Métro lines to 'pneu' operation, but an exception was made for line 6, which has much more open-air running (mostly on viaduct) than any other Métro line. This gave much noise and vibration with the old Sprague stock and this line was therefore an ideal candidate for rubber-tyred trains, assisted by the fact that the track on line 6 needed replacing anyway. Track conversion commenced in 1972 and new rolling stock of type **MP73** and comprising 252 cars was built by CIMT with ANF bogies and Jeumont equipment. Surprisingly, for a rubber-tyred line, the rolling stock was introduced within the space of just a month – from July 1974 (the period of the year with the lowest peak traffic) with extra trains added in time for maximum winter service, which starts in October. Trains were formed into five cars: M-B-A-N-M. The bodywork design was based on the already successful MF67 stock (q.v. below), which by then had become the accepted design for new stock until the advent of the MF77 type. The cars were numbered as follows:

M3501–3602 N4501–4550 A6501–6550 B7001–7050

Some trains of MP73 stock were subsequently allocated to line 11 from January 1976, to supplement the MP55 trains and providing an increased service on that line. The MP73 sets on line 11 operate in four-car formation like their MP55 counterparts, with the spare (fifth) cars being stored. A small number of MP73 train sets also operated on line 4 between 1975 and 1979.

The MP73 stock can thus mostly be found on line 6 and as this line contains several open-air sections, amounting to almost half the line's length, special features were incorporated in these trains. This includes weatherproof ventilation, windscreen wipers, grooved tyres, snowproof resistance grids and chassis parts in Corten rustproof alloy instead of steel. This was the first new stock for the Paris Métro to be delivered in the new royal blue and white livery, with a dark blue stripe at waist level, and first class indicated by a yellow band at roof line. Outside door indicator lights are fitted to these trains, after an experiment with a train of MP59 stock on line 4 (3231–4213–6001–(7004)–4214–3232) which incorporated an MP73 trailer.

Much of the Métro follows the line of the street, including the open-air sections of line 6, which accounts for the sharp curves above and below ground. An MP73 stock train approaches Sèvres Lecourbe heading for Charles de Gaulle – Étoile. *Brian Hardy*

It is interesting to note that M3599/3600 served as prototypes for the Marseille Métro, and M3602 for the Lyon Métro. In addition, cars A6550 and N4550, both having experimental suspension, first entered service on line 1 with the MP59 stock and were painted in the old livery of that stock, while the rest of the MP73 type was in the royal blue and white livery. Both cars were repainted into standard colours when they went into service on line 6 in 1976.

The current MP73 stock fleet comprises 246 cars, six of which have been scrapped (N4550, A6504, A6541, A6550, B7002 and B7004).

In 1997 the RATP refurbished one train of MP73 stock on line 6 (M3557–B7029–A6529–N4529–M3558), prior to the complete renovation of the fleet. As with other already refurbished trains, the interiors were fitted with individual vandal-proof seats and the exteriors were painted in the new colours with the front being black under the cab window. Following trials in service, refurbishment of the MP73 stock began in September 1998 with the work being shared with Cannes La Bocca Industries and the RATP's own workshops at Fontenay (line 1) and Boissy (RER line A). The first refurbished train returned to line 6 in April 1999. So that a working 'float' of trains could be provided for the work, without reducing the train services on line 6, the transfer of MP59 stock four-car refurbished sets to line 11 was completed in early-1999. This enabled the four-car MP73 sets on line 11 to be reduced to three trains.

Refurbished trains of MP73 stock have begun entering service on line 6, following a prototype undertaken by the RATP in 1997. In common with other refurbished trains the cab end is painted black. *RATP*

The MF67 Stock

While the success of the rubber-tyred stock was undoubted, it took approximately three years to convert the trackwork and generally about another year to phase in the rolling stock. At that rate it would have been impossible to have completed the modernisation of the Métro until into the 21st century. Between 1951 and 1964 there were, too, considerable advances in the design of conventional rapid transit trains in other countries, and in 1964 the RATP began to study the development of modern rolling stock which would provide the same acceleration and braking characteristics, as well as the quiet and comfortable ride, as the 'pneu' trains. The result was the **MF67** stock, the first train of which went into service on line 3 on 21 December 1967.

Externally, the MF67 stock differed from the 'pneu' trains only in the restyled front end and driver's cab, and in its pull-down opening saloon windows instead of sliding vents. The trains are much quieter than the Classic stock – some have rubber sandwich wheels, a ring of rubber blocks being pressed between the steel tyres and the rims of the wheels. Rubber springing in the bogies and sound insulation of the bodies also contribute to the reduction of noise.

The MF67 cars had all axles driven and originally the trains were formed of motor cars only, to give a performance approximate to that of the 'pneu' stock. Half the cars have monomotor bogies with a 194hp motor and half have two-motor bogies with two 99hp motors. Control is by servo-motors to give smooth acceleration. Service braking is rheostatic down to low speeds with air taking over thereafter. In practice, the provision of all-motor-car trains proved to be over-generous and trailers were subsequently introduced in 1974. Normal train formation is now three motor cars and two trailers in a five car set. Modifications introduced on successive batches of motor cars include regenerative braking, mechanical ventilation disc brakes and air suspension. Internally, the MF67 stock has generous lighting by fluorescent tubes and comfortable leatherette seating. Some of the prototypes, however, have a different cosmetic finish. Loudspeakers allow the driver to address the passengers and the MF67E stock on line 2 has been modified so that there is two-way communication between the driver and passengers should an emergency handle be operated, a feature first adopted on the MF77 trains. Door indicator lights are fitted to the car exteriors, so that staff can easily identify faulty doors.

Whilst in general terms the MF67 type is grouped into six sub classes, (generally - designated MF67A to MF67F) when analysed in depth there are in fact 15 different types, each having slight differences, generally in equipment, but sometimes in cosmetic finishes. For example, one train was delivered in unpainted aluminium and stainless steel. This saved 700kg per car, but increased productions costs meant the design was not pursued.

Following the entry into service of the first (prototype) train (type 'W1') on line 3 in December 1967, production started of the 'A' series, entering service on line 3 from August 1968, formed into five-car all motor car trains: M-N-NA-N-M. The order also comprised the unpainted/stainless steel train (type 'W2') and six single cars of types 'B1' and 'B2'. The 'A' series comprised two types – the 'A1' with monomotor bogies and the 'A2' with bi-motor bogies. The last of this series went into service on line 3 in January 1970, making a total of 42 five-car trains, including the prototypes and the experimental cars. The next line to receive MF67 stock was line 7 from June 1971. Prior to this, a new series of MF67 stock commenced delivery – the 'C1' – from early-1971, first entering service on line 3 from April. This allowed the release of the 'A2' type from line 3 to line 7 and from December 1971 a further new batch of type 'C2' entered service directly on line 7, the last to do so being in January 1974. This segregated the stocks so that the trains with monomotor bogies were all on line 3 and those with bi-motors were on line 7. All three types 'A', 'B' and 'C' and their variations were built by CIMT and Brissonneau et Lotz.

Included in the prototype cars and trains were two trailers, one of which was finished in unpainted aluminium/stainless steel. These two trailers entered service in late

1969 and early 1970 to evaluate the performance of trains that were not formed of all motor cars, being transferred to line 7 in November 1971.

The dilution of train sets with trailers was successful and it allowed the RATP to reduce both capital and operating costs. The next order for MF67 stock therefore comprised all trailers – both driving and non-driving – built jointly by Alsthom and SFB from mid-1974 to early 1976, the first examples entering service on line 3 in September 1974 (trailers) and on line 9 (driving trailers). These trailers (156 driving trailers coded 'S' [sans moteurs, without motors], 145 second class trailers coded 'B' and 62 first class trailers coded 'A') were known as MF67 type'D'. A carefully prepared plan involving the reformation of the all-motor sets on lines 3 and 7 was implemented. On line 3, the two 'N' cars were removed and replaced by 'B' trailers, giving a formation of M-B-NA-B-M. On line 7, one 'N' and one 'NA' was removed and replaced by a new 'B' and 'A' respectively, giving a formation of M-B-A-N-M. The new driving trailers ('S') were formed with displaced 'N' and 'NA' cars forming trains thus: S-N-NA-N-S. These went into service on lines 9 and 13, with a small allocation to line 10 to supplement the articulated stock then being transferred from line 13. To complete this plan, four non driving motors (N11131–11134) were converted to first class accommodation, becoming NA12129–12132 in 1974. It is interesting to note that the MF67D stock had to be delivered in the old pale blue livery (first class cars cream) to match the older cars of MF67 stock that they were being formed with, even though previous new stock (the MP73 for line 6) had been delivered in the new royal blue and white livery.

Line 3 was the first recipient of the first of the new generation steel-wheel-on-steel-rail trains of MF67 stock. A train in original livery is seen at the eastern terminus of line 3 at Gallieni, to where it was extended in 1971. *John Herting*

One of the few Métro trains not to have received the new green and white livery is the MF67W2 prototype, seen in Vaugirard depot on line 12. This train has seen periods of intermittent use in passenger service, the last on line 9, but is more usually used for instructional purposes.
Julian Pepinster

A further two batches of MF67 stock were yet to be built, but these were not generally to be mixed with the A-D type. The next batch was the MF67 type 'E' and these five car trains in the new livery from new were built by CIMT and entered service on line 8 from 14 July 1975, with some going to line 13. The delivery of this stock to line 8 allowed some of the grey Sprague stock to be transferred to line 2 (and later, lines 9 and 12), then seeing the end of two-motor Sprague stock on line 2 on 22 March 1976.

The final batch of MF67 stock was the type 'F' built by BL. These trains, also five cars in length, had interior fans fitted for improved ventilation and they were instantly recognisable from the outside, by having a smoother finish to the roof line. They first entered service on line 13 from October 1976, displacing the MF67E type on that line, to join their sister cars on line 8.

The MF67E/F batches of 1975-76 were delivered in the new blue and white livery and subsequent repaints of the original trains saw this livery applied. A train of the MF67A-C type awaits departure from Mairie de Montreuil on line 9.
Brian Hardy

Interior view of MF67 stock when working on line 3bis and before refurbishment. Vandal resistant seats had been fitted by this time.
Brian Hardy

The interior of the MF67C2A proto-type on line 9, which is the only train on the line not to have been refurbished. This served as a proto-type for the MF67F trains and was fitted with roof level fans. The interior colour scheme of this train was not adopted.
Brian Hardy

Interior of refurbished MF67 stock, with the interior colour scheme predominantly green. The refurbished trains on line 3bis are finished similarly.
Brian Hardy

The last batch of stock of type MF67 was the MF67F delivered in 1976-78. It has seen service on lines 7, 7bis and 13 but all of it can now be found on line 5, as seen here at Quai de la Rapée. This type and the MF67E are unlikely to be refurbished because of their condition after years of open-air running and (for line 5) stabling, and will probably be the first to be scrapped.
Brian Hardy

With the advent of the MF77 stock, which first went to line 13, the displaced MF67F trains were transferred to line 7, which allowed the diluted M-B-A-N-M formations of the A-D type to be transferred to lines 9 and 12. In fact both these lines operated formations of M-B-A-N-M and S-N-NA-N-S. Some of the latter driving trailer sets also went to line 5 from April 1978, and to line 2 from February 1979.

Deliveries of the MF77 stock then went to lines 7 (from September 1979) and 8 (from July 1980), which released the MF67F from line 7 to go to line 5, and the MF67E from line 8 to line 2. The earlier A-D types on line 2 went to line 12, finishing off the Sprague stock on that line in December 1980, followed by line 2 in June 1981. Enough MF67F trains were available from line 7 to replace the Sprague stock on line 7bis from July 1980, which operated in full-length five-car formations, while from mid-1981 a sufficient number of MF67E trains were available to replace the Sprague stock on line 3bis, but in three-car formations, the other two cars of the set being stored. To give a section of first class accommodation on these three-car sets, a small portion of the middle trailer was converted as such and were temporarily classified as 'Ba'. This arrangement on the two branch lines was short-lived and a more permanent stock situation was established. From February 1982, the five-car trains of MF67F stock on line 7bis were transferred back to line 7 (and subsequently to line 5), being replaced by four-car sets of MF67E from line 3bis, the first class trailer in the formation being brought out of store. On line 3bis, three-car trains of MF67A-D type were transferred in from line 9, in the formation of M-Ba-M.

The open-air stabling of the MF67F trains on line 5 at Bobigny from 1985 soon highlighted corrosion problems in the door pocket areas on these trains and thus between 1987 and 1989 all were modified at Vaugirard depot with enclosed windows at the door slide-back positions, giving a 'double-glazed' appearance. In each seating area of the saloon, a narrow section for window opening was provided.

Recent changes to the MF67 stock fleet have been very few. However, some conversions of car types has taken place. On line 9, MF67C2A cars N11005 and NA12003 have been de-motored to become trailers B14159 and A13073 respectively, while A13069, A13067 and A13061 have become (respectively) B14156-B14158. MF67E motor car M10310, which was used for testing experimental traction equipment, has been converted to a driving trailer and renumbered S9167. In addition, N11226 has been withdrawn.

With some of the MF67 stock over 25 years old, it was necessary to consider the refurbishment of some cars. Motor car M10226 became the prototype in 1993 following which it was decided that the trains on line 9 would be refurbished. The order was split so that ACC at Clermont Ferrand and Cannes La Bocca Industries each refurbished 24 trains, while the RATP refurbished 22 trains at Boissy (RER) workshops. The first completed train entered service on line 9 on 29 August 1995, the project being complete in March 1998. Refurbishment of the six three-car trains on line 3bis began in the spring of 1997, the last being completed in August 1998. Cars M10104 and B14036 on line 3 have also been refurbished in 1998 with longitudinal seating, as a trial pending refurbishment of the remainder of the MF67 fleet on that line. The MF67 stock can now be found in service on seven Métro lines, in the following formations (reference to former first class cars (A and NA) is now superfluous:

	Type	Normal Formation	Variations
Line 2	MF67E	M-B-A-N-M	
Line 3	MF67A-D	M-B-NA-B-M	M-N-NA-N-M (two trains)
Line 3bis	MF67C-D	M-B-M	
Line 5	MF67F	M-B-A-N-M	
Line 9	MF67A-D	M-B-NA-N-M	
	MF67A-D	S-N-NA-N-S	
Line 10	MF67A-D	S-N-NA-N-S	S-N-N-N-S (one train)
	MF67E	M-B-A-N-M	
Line 12	MF67A-D	S-N-NA-N-S	M-N-NA-N-S (one train)

SUMMARY OF VEHICLES IN STOCK – MF67 SERIES

Stock Type	M	N	NA	A	B	S	Total
MF67 W1	2	2	1	—	1	—	6
MF67 W2	2	2	1	—	1	—	6
MF67 A1	36	40	20	—	—	—	96
MF67 A2	39	39	20	—	—	—	98
MF67 B1	4	—	—	—	—	—	4
MF67 B2	1	1	—	—	—	—	2
MF67 C1	44	40	26	—	—	—	110
MF67 C1A	2	2	1	—	—	—	5
MF67 C2	91	91	46	—	—	—	228
MF67 C2A	2	1	—	1	1	—	5
MF67 CS	2	1	1	—	—	—	4
MF67 CX	—	7	9	—	—	—	16
MF67D	—	—	—	59	148	156	363
MF67E	113	56	—	56	56	1	282
MF67F	104	51	—	51	51	—	257
Total:	442	333	125	167	258	157	1482

The MF77 stock

The extension of the Métro into the suburbs of Paris and the greater distance between stations on these extensions (800 to 1,000m as against about 500m in the City area) highlighted some of the weak points of existing designs and in 1972 the RATP instituted studies for the design of rolling stock which would be faster and more comfortable than existing trains, and more suited to suburban work. Experiments with various features, such as plug doors, internal decor etc., were made on various cars of MF67 stock and research was undertaken by industrial designers, acting in collaboration with both engineers and marketing specialists, and backed by surveys made among the travelling public to find out what they wanted in the new trains. A mock-up coach was built and exhibited at the 75th anniversary of the Métro at Porte Maillot station in 1975 which was in green and brown livery. The result of all this was the **MF77** stock, the first train of which entered service on line 13 in September 1978. The trains are formed into five-car sets (M-B-NA-B-M) and can now be found operating the complete services on lines 7, 8 and 13.

When the new trains appeared they showed an advance in design not only over existing Métro stock, but also over trains running on rapid transit systems elsewhere. The sides of the cars are not straight, unlike all previous Métro stock, but curve outwards to give the maximum width at waist level consistent with the constraints of the loading gauge. This, together with the use of plug-type doors instead of ones sliding back into recesses, has given a total increase in width of 140mm at the shoulder level of seated passengers. The unusual (for Paris Métro) shape of the cars was set off by a striking livery of off-white, relieved only by dark blue panels round the windscreens of driving motor cars. First class accommodation was indicated by a yellow band at cant rail level. The cars are also slightly longer (15.110m on motor cars and 15.120m on trailers and non-driving motor cars) and in fact at some of the shorter stations, the head of the train is actually in the tunnel during stops. The new cars have only three pairs of doors per side as against four in the previous stocks, but the door openings are much wider, at 1.575m instead of 1.30m, thus allowing a rapid flow of passengers. Push-button door control, comprising a button concealed in a shell grip, allows passengers to open individual pairs of doors once the train has stopped at a station, rather than by lifting a latch as hitherto.

The next generation of steel-wheel-on-steel rail rolling stock was the MF77, which was purpose-built for higher speeds on longer suburban routes. This is at Bastille on line 8 and shows the train formation number (124) on the car end, used to identify train positions at stabling locations. The letter 'G' appended indicates that it is fitted with rail greasing equipment. *Capital Transport*

The interiors of the MF77 stock were quite bright when new, but the roof grilles do not lend themselves to easy cleaning and the interiors are not as smart as they originally were. Also, many of the end windows have frosted over, which prevents a view through to the adjacent car. It is expected that when refurbishment of this stock commences in the new Millennium, attention will focus on improving the car lighting arrangements. *Capital Transport*

Internally, the MF77 trains are distinguished by a harmony of muted tones, in contrast to the striking colour schemes favoured for other contemporary stock elsewhere. The seat colour is dark blue, walls are light blue and the doors, grab rails etc, are finished in stainless steel. The floors are covered with rubber matting. The space between the seats has been increased from 48cm to 54cm, to give improved comfort to seated passengers. All the materials used in the interior furnishings are, or have been treated to be, fire resistant. Lighting is by fluorescent tubes but, to reduce glare, is placed behind grilles which run the length of the ceiling and incorporate fans for ventilation. Seating is provided by individual pairs of seats instead of pairs of benches, and those at the non driving ends of the car are arranged in groups of three to face each other, giving the effect of a small saloon. The former tip-up perches have been replaced by proper folding seats, just as comfortable as the main seating. Heating and ventilation is thermostatically controlled. In addition to the windows in the communicating doors between the cars, windows are also provided either side of these at the trailing ends. This helped create an atmosphere of spaciousness and a feeling of security which, with the high standard of design, gave a pleasant and relaxing effect overall. However, over the years, the glass in the end windows has become 'frosted' and no longer is it possible to see through to the next car, unless a breakage has caused a replacement.

The car body is made of light alloy sections, giving a saving of over two tonnes in weight over a comparable train of steel construction. The driving cabs of the train were designed after considerable ergonomic study and are laid out in such a way as to afford maximum convenience and comfort to the drivers. As on all modern stock, a high-frequency telephone link keeps the driver in touch with the Control Centre (PCC), but an innovation on the MF77 stock is a two-way link between the driver and passengers, which comes into action when the emergency alarm signal has been actuated, in addition to the normal public address equipment.

MF77 trailer B32268 on line 8. Note the end window, which has either escaped the 'frosting over' process or has been replaced. 'Créteil' is illuminated in blue to the right of the double doors. *Capital Transport*

87

The MF77 trains were built by SFB and Alsthom, the main order comprising 187 five-car trains, between 1978 and 1982. A further order for ten trains was built by Alsthom in 1986, to provide the stock required for the extensions to line 7. The MF77 trains are fitted with MTE-type bogies of the type already in use on the MF67F trains. Equipment is provided by TCO. There are six motor bogies on each five-car train and each motor bogie has a 266kW motor installed lengthwise between the two axles, in the centre of the bogie frame. On motor cars there is a regenerative braking, plus air brakes, while on trailers, braking is by compressed air alone.

Traction and braking control is performed by thyristor-equipped current choppers. The choppers do away with rheostats, which had hitherto been used to start the motors. They ensure far greater operating versatility and also cut down consumption while enabling power to be recovered on braking furnished by the motors operating as generators, which is fed back to the power line. Thus, the energy saving on a line equipped with modern cars can reach 40% compared with conventional trains with rheostatic starting and devoid of regenerative braking. In this way, the energy which was unnecessarily dissipated as heat is now recovered, the temperature in the Métro is reduced and comfort is enhanced.

The first train of MF77 stock was made available to the press at the SFB factory in Valenciennes on 25 October 1977 and a car was exhibited outside Galéries Lafayette department store in the same month. In December the stock was exhibited to the public at Châtelet – les Halles station on the RER. The first train to be delivered to Vaugirard depot arrived on 23 June 1978, and underwent exhaustive testing. Deliveries allowed the first train to enter service on line 13 on 22 September 1978. The following year line 7 was the next recipient of the MF77 stock, although it was not until 1985 that the last of the MF67F type was transferred away from line 7 to line 5. Line 13 had all MF77 trains by the end of 1979. In 1980 line 8 began to receive MF77 stock, replacing the MF67E type. The last train of the main order of MF77 stock entered service on 2 February 1983 and subsequently allowed, through cascades of other stock, the last of the Sprague stock to be withdrawn.

The additional ten trains of MF77 stock for line 7 extensions and service enhancements were delivered between September 1985 and July 1986, all entering service (on line 13, with other MF77 trains transferred to line 7) during 1986.

Built by SFB:

M30001–30074	B32001–32074	NA31001–31037
M30119–30158	B32119–32158	NA31060–31079
M30219–30252	B32219–32252	NA31110–31126
M30295–30328	B32295–32328	NA31148–31164
M30365–30370	B32365–32370	NA31183–31185

Built by Alsthom:

M30075–30118	B32075–32118	NA31038–31059
M30159–30218	B32159–32218	NA31080–31109
M30253–30294	B32253–32294	NA31127–31147
M30329–30364	B32329–32364	NA31165–31182
M30371–30374	B32371–32374	NA31186–31187
M30375–30394*	B32375–32394*	NA31188–31197*

Note* 1985–86 batch.
M30154 and B32154 were scrapped April 1984.

The MF77 trains on lines 7, 8 and 13 are to have a mid-life refurbishment. Technical changes will see modernised rheostatic braking and ATO equipment and the fitting of air conditioning. More visible to the public, the interior car lighting will be redesigned and will see the end of the 'metal net' which currently causes difficulties in lighting maintenance and cleaning.

The prototype 'BOA' as seen in Vaugirard depot while still under test. It was fitted with steerable axles. The train saw a short spell in passenger service on line 5 in the off-peaks but is now stored pending a decision on its future. It did, however, provide the necessary data to enable the small build of nine trains of MF88 stock for line 7bis. *Jeanne Hardy*

The MF88 Stock

Not content with the successful MF77 class previously described, the RATP continued planning for future Métro rolling stock of the steel-wheel-on-steel-rail type. The results of studies and tests was the 'BOA', a fully articulated train using single axles instead of bogies, thus providing the train with steered axles without the extra weight and complication of a steerable bogie. The first prototype train was designed and built by the RATP themselves in Vaugirard depot from 1980 and consisted of three 10m articulated cars with monomoteur axles. Apart from the articulation and the interconnection between axles, all parts used were already on other stocks, being well-tried and tested. For instance the underfloor equipment is as used on MP73 stock, and the car bodies were most definitely MF77.

Tests recommenced in February 1985, the new innovation being a great success. With the reduction in the weight of the train, it consumed less current and stress on curves was much reduced. It was also tested on the very sharp non-passenger loop at Porte Dauphine on line 2 without problems. Early in 1986 the system was adapted to have steerable axles at the front of the train instead of bogies, whereby the leading axle 'reads' the curvature of the track and then guides the second axle. The leading axle is non-load-bearing and has smaller wheels than on all other axles.

Following on from these tests, the next stage was to develop a train which would ultimately carry passengers and the original 'BOA' was returned to Vaugirard workshops to enable a four-bodied train to be constructed. This enabled three different types of body articulation to be tested, one each by Faiveley, ANF and Alsthom. That by Faiveley comprised an elastic assembly made of rubber with distortable joints, the ANF example having a distortable assembly made of rigid and flexible frames and the Alsthom (RATP Patent) articulated gangway had a rigid assembly articulated at both ends between car bodies. The last two articulations each contained seats and the Alsthom gangway incorporated side windows. All seats were of the tip-up type. The four-body section thus allowed complete intercirculation by passengers.

The driving motor cars were 12.19m long and the non-driving motors 10.98m long, making the four-body train 46.34m long overall. Tests resumed in 1987 and subsequently it was decided that it would operate on trial on line 5. Empty running commenced on 12 November 1990 and passengers were carried for the first time on 31 December 1990. Because the train was much shorter than normal-length trains on line 5 and because it was not equipped for automatic driving, its operation was confined to off-peak periods Mondays to Fridays. Also being tested at the same time was the use of asynchronous motors on this train, following trials on MF77 driving motor car M30125 and MF67 cars M10024 and M10025.

The BOA train, which was given the numbers M30411-N11552-N11553-M30412, was thus been the testbed and prototype for the future **MF88** stock for line 7bis, which ultimately allowed, through consequential inter-line stock transfers, the withdrawal of the articulated MA52 stock. The BOA is now stored, pending a decision on its role in connection with future rolling stock experiments.

To operate the complete service on line 7bis, nine trains of MF88 stock were built, following on from trials with the BOA, entering service from 1994. Because the trains have steerable axles and line 7bis has sharp curves, these trains tend to 'bounce' their way along. Formed into three-car trains there is complete intercirculation for passengers through the train. This is at Pré-Saint-Gervais on the loop, which acts as the terminal station, where trains stand for time. *Brian Hardy*

The first three-car train of the production MF88 stock was delivered to Bobigny depot by road in late December 1992, the other eight trains following at lengthy intervals until June 1994. They are formed into three-car sets with complete intercirculation by passengers throughout. These were the first new trains to be delivered in the new RATP corporate colours of white and green, with a partial black front. Unlike previous types of stock, the car and door windows are much deeper. The main transverse seats were not tip-up, as on the BOA, but the under seat area was kept clear for easier cleaning access.

Four trains were available to enter service from 24 January 1994 but the last did not enter service until October 1994. Because this small fleet of trains is allocated to line 7bis, a small maintenance workshop has been opened at Pre-Saint-Gervais, on the track formerly served by the erstwhile shuttle service to Porte des Lilas.

The MF88 stock began a new system of car numbering. Hitherto, it had always been the practice of preceding the number with a letter which denoted the type of car. With the MF88 stock (and subsequently the MP89), the year of order prefixed the identification letter and vehicle number. Numbers were allocated thus:

88 M 001–018   Driving Motor Cars
88 B 001–009   Trailers

Interior of the MF88 stock, looking through from one motor car to the adjacent trailer. Note that all the seats are fixed to the car sides, giving uninterrupted access underneath them for cleaning. *Jeanne Hardy*

By the end of March 1999, about half of the trains on line 1 were operated by MP89 stock, the refurbished trains of MP59 stock that they replaced being transferred to line 4. At the eastern terminus of Château de Vincennes, unit CC05 is seen in the arrival platforms. Recently, the 'unit' numbers have been repositioned between the head and tail lights, without the 'CC' prefix.
Brian Hardy

The MP89 Stock

The need to replace the original rubber-tyred trains of MP55 stock on line 11 led to a new generation of 'pneu' trains being developed – the **MP89** type. At the same time, new trains for the new Météor line were required and it was decided that trains of a similar type would be built for both. The main difference between the two types lay in the method of operation on their respective lines. Those on Météor would be totally automatic with no train staff on board (MP89CA) and those for use on conventional lines with manual or automatic (ATO) driving (MP89CC).

It should be remembered that line 1's fleet of MP59 trains were refurbished in the period 1989–1992 and that work was coupled with the future order for new trains in mind. The plan resulted in the following:

- 52 trains of MP89 stock to be built for line 1.
- 52 trains of refurbished MP59 stock to be transferred from line 1 to line 4.

Along with the above was the desire to scrap the MP55 stock and to replace it, further (four-car) trains of MP59 stock on line 4 were refurbished. This resulted in:

- 22 four-car trains of refurbished MP59 stock to be transferred to line 11 with the two unrefurbished cars in each six-car set being scrapped.
- The MP55 stock scrapped.
- 27 six-car trains of unrefurbished MP59 stock on line 4 to be scrapped.

The order for the MP89 stock was placed with GEC Alsthom (now Alstom) in October 1990 and comprised the 52 six-car trains for line 1 and, initially, 19 six-car trains for line 14 (Météor). Two further trains for line 14 are to be delivered for the one-station extension from Madeleine to Saint-Lazare, with an option for a further 22 trains as the various planned extensions come to fruition.

Part of the delay in the MP89 stock design being finalised was caused by the desire to have inter-circulation for passengers and to find a system that would negotiate the sharp curves in the Bastille area, the sharpest on the Métro system. The finished product is illustrated on this departing westbound train. *Brian Hardy*

This is how the first trains were delivered – with conventional inner car ends and locked communicating doors. Whilst testing began immediately, it took time to perfect the intercirculation between cars. This photo is at the Valenciennes factory on 24 January 1995. The initial trains were returned to the factory to be modified before entering passenger service. *RATP*

The trains of MP89 stock built for line 14 (Météor) are quite similar to those on line 1, but lack a driver's cab, although a full driving desk (normally locked out of use) is provided. This view is at the future station of Olympiades, but until it opens to the public in 2005, it is being used as a two-track maintenance depot. Because line 14 is totally automatic with no train staff on board, there is no need for unit numbers or train set numbers. *RATP*

Both types of MP89 stock are visually similar, the main difference being that a driver's cab is provided at the outer ends of the MP89CC for line 1. On the MP89CA there is no driving cab and passengers have an unrestricted view of the line ahead, with three longitudinal seats per side. There are, however, full driving facilities provided behind a locked cabinet. The train formations on each line are identical, with the outer end cars being driving trailers and the four intermediate cars being non-driving motor cars. The formation is thus S-N-N-N-N-S. As with the previous new build of stock, the MF88, car numbers are comprise the stock type (89), car type (S or N) and then the car number. Those on line 1 are numbered '001' upwards and those on line 14 '1001' upwards. At a later date, should traffic increase as predicted, the trains on line 14 will be increased to eight cars, by the addition of another non driving motor car (N) and a trailer (B).

The first train, one of two prototypes for Météor, was launched at the Valenciennes factory on 8 February 1995 and was delivered in April 1995. The first train for line 1 was delivered in September 1995. The first train of both types were delivered with normally-locked communicating doors between cars, but it was the intention that all six cars should be accessible to passengers from whichever point they board the train. This was realised by the time they entered service but the solution was more problematical on line 1 with its sharp curves at Bastille. Faiveley provided the through gangways on line 14 while a Swiss company provided those for the trains on line 1. The original trains returned to the manufacturer to be suitably modified.

Each car has three wide externally-hung double doors per side and slide back against the car body. All doors on the train are under control of the driver for both opening and closing. Features perpetuated from the MF88 stock include deep saloon and door windows.

Left At first glance, the interiors of the MP89 stock are similar. However, there are some differences. On the trains for line 1, most seating provided in the driving trailer cars is in the 2+1 arrangement, but there is normal 2+2 seating in the intermediate cars, as can be seen in the distance beyond the gangway. As well as grab rails above head height for standing passengers, the floor-to-ceiling grab poles incorporate a three-pole arrangement, enabling a more comfortable stand. *RATP*

Right The interior of MP89 stock on line 14 shows that the seating is arranged 2+1, apart from around the car end gangways, which has longitudinal seating. Above each gangway, closed circuit TV is provided, to enable in-car monitoring from the control centre, because no staff would normally be found on the train. In other respects the interiors are the same. *Capital Transport*

Seats inside the car are arranged transversely in the 2+1 configuration on line 14 to give more standing space, as they are on the driving trailers on line 1. The seats in the intermediate non-driving motor cars on line 1, however, are in the normal 2+2 arrangement. The seats are hung against the bodyside, to enable full access for floor cleaning. Adjacent to the through gangways are groups of three longitudinal seats on each side. Because the trains on line 14 are completely automatic and operate without any staff, two cameras are provided per car, enabling the control centre (PCC) to monitor the interiors.

The non-driving motor cars have welded frame monomotor bogies with air bag secondary pneumatic suspension, with three-phase asynchronous motors. Power control is by GTO voltage inverters controlled through microprocessors. Regenerative braking is provided, along with standard air brakes on the steel wheels as a back-up.

The first train of MP89 stock entered service on line 1 on 27 February 1997 and as at the end of March 1999, a total of 30 trains had been commissioned for service.

MF 2000

The MF67 stock is now around 30 years old and the RATP have been developing the steel-wheel-on-steel-rail train for the future. Dubbed the MF2000, it is currently expected that this stock will replace all the MF67 type between 2005 and 2020, although a prototype train is expected in 2001 for evaluation, prior to the details of the main order being finalised. The new five-car sets will continue with passenger access throughout and will have deep saloon and door windows. The cabs will have gently sloping fronts and will be ergonomically designed to give maximum benefit for the driver.

The first lines to receive the new trains are expected to be 2, 5 and 9. The trains on lines 2 and 5 are the newer MF67 trains but these are unlikely to be refurbished and will be the first to be replaced because of bodywork corrosion through open-air running. The 70 refurbished trains on line 9 will be sufficient to replace all the stock on lines 10 and 12, the former possibly in four-car formation. Later deliveries will then concentrate on replacing the refurbished trains on lines 3, 10 and 12.

All-Over-Advertisements

In July 1998, the RATP began using Métro rolling stock for all-over-advertising, presumably following on the practice started on the London Underground in 1995. Unlike London, however, whose all-over-adverts contracts were for a year or more, those on the Métro were for short periods only of around two weeks. Only those which were applied during the 1998 World Cup were for longer periods. Advertisements have included FNAC (Department store selling books, records films and hi-fi equipment), Soupline (a fabric softener) and Snickers (chocolate bar). This was unusual in that the advert pictures themselves depicted sports images – the chocolate bar is supposed to give one more energy to partake in sporting activities! Some of the advertising cars have also included a local or national cultural event, such as 'Printemps du Quebec', for which an all-over advert train of MP59 stock ran on line 1.

Trains used for advertising has included MF67 and MF77 and 'pneu' MP59 stock. Whilst all-over-advertising liveries are often a contentious subject when applied on rolling stock, especially when a corporate livery is otherwise rigidly adhered to, there is no doubt that advertising using trains generates money that the authorities would not have been able to do.

Although all-over advertisements have been around on buses for many years, they are fairly new to Underground trains. On the Métro in Paris, adverts usually last for short periods only. This train of MP59 stock operated on line 1 in the spring of 1999 and is seen at Bastille on 22 March 1999.
Brian Hardy

Even the erstwhile MP55 stock on line 11 carried all-over-adverts during the World Cup Championships in 1998. Former composite trailer AB5506 poses at Châtelet on 20 May 1998. *RATP*

CHAPTER 6

Métro Operations

Signalling

As far as can be ascertained, line 1 was opened for traffic without the protection of signals of any kind. As there were only ten trains operating on a ten or twelve minute headway, a time interval system apparently sufficed. However, on 20 September 1900, a new timetable doubled the service and it seems that this coincided with the adoption of a full system of signalling.

The first system to be adopted was the Hall block system, a mechanical one in which the signals were set by the passage of trains. The leading wheel of the first coach depressed a treadle at the side of the track and this in turn activated the signal arm, causing a disc to move and change the signal to caution (green). It also changed the last signal but one to clear (white) A green signal could be passed at caution speed. Not surprisingly, this was open to abuse and on 19 October 1900 there was a rear end collision between Champs-Élysées and Concorde, when a train set back and was run into by a following one, which was running under clear signals. Fortunately, there was no serious injury to passengers or crew. The green signal indications were kept as permissive 'slowdown' signals (equivalent of the present yellow) and red 'compulsory stop' signals were created. It was forbidden to pass a red signal unless on a written order, and then at only 10kph. When line 2 (Nord) was opened, the system was modified further and the signals remained normally at red, clearing to white only immediately in front of a train and so avoiding any confusion with street lamps on the overhead section. The elevated part of line 2 Sud used semaphore signals similar to those of the main line railways. With careful maintenance, the Hall system worked quite well, but the trackside treadles were very easily put out of alignment and its use was not further extended after the opening of line 3.

Its successor was known as the Métro automatic block system. In this, a bar about five metres long was placed parallel to the running rails, on the opposite side of the track to the third rail. When energised by contact with the collector shoe of a passing train, the bar transmitted an electrical impulse, changing the signal to clear or danger as required. The system was installed on lines 4 to 8 as they were opened, and between 1914 and 1918 replaced the Hall signalling on lines 1, 2 (Nord and Sud) and 3.

The Nord-Sud company, ever independent, made use of an entirely different system based on track circuits and relays. The entry of a train into a section caused a short circuit and cut off current from the relays, putting the signal at danger behind the train. It remained so until the train had cleared the next section ahead. At stations, three aspect signals were used, a green distant allowing entry to the station at reduced speed as soon as the preceding train had left. At the exits from stations, there were two red indications and one white, one red being extinguished to allow departure when a train ahead had cleared the first section. The three aspect signals were ultimately introduced on the CMP, but the track circuits were given up in 1932, two years after the Nord-Sud was taken over.

From 1921, the CMP had in fact adopted a very similar system, but using alternating current for the track circuits rather than direct current. Unlike both the previous Métro block and the Nord-Sud systems, signals were normally clear, and changed to danger only with the passage of a train. The system was first used on line 9, and all other lines had been converted to it by 1942. Relays with proving contacts were used from 1928 onwards to provide added safety.

After 1945, it was necessary to renew the signalling and the opportunity was taken to adopt the internationally-accepted colours of red, yellow and green. Green distant signals were replaced by yellow aspects in March 1955 and in turn, green replaced white as the 'line clear' indication in April of the same year. More recently, the adoption of continuously-welded rail had made it necessary to adopt high-frequency current at different frequencies in adjacent sections, for the signalling.

Today, the normal signal on the Métro is the two aspect colour light block (or 'spacing') signal, giving a green or red aspect according to the track circuit. At the entry to busier stations, three aspect signals are often found, in which a yellow indication allows entry at reduced speed when the preceding train has just cleared it. In certain places, this signal is supplemented by a preceding intermediate signal, whose function is to anticipate the clearing of the station and which, when clear, allows a train to approach a station when the rear of the preceding train is half-way along the platform. These signals are generally protected by an outer two aspect signal, which remains at red when the others have cleared. On curves and other areas of reduced visibility, repeater signals are provided, giving yellow and green aspects only and are worked in conjunction with the block signal ahead. In all cases, a train is protected in the rear by two red signals, except at entry to stations as mentioned above.

Although trainstops were never used on the Métro, from the days since the Hall signalling system, a train which passed a signal at danger set off a bell and visual indication at the next station. These were acknowledged only by station staff and such incidents were reported in writing. This system disappeared some 15–20 years ago, with the abolition of platform staff, being replaced by the CMC system (q.v.).

There were few shunting signals in the early days, but a system developed as terminal layouts grew more complex, quite independent of the running signals. Following a collision at Porte des Lilas in 1949, when a driver confused a shunting signal with a block signal and passed the latter at red, block signals have generally been removed from these areas, leaving only the shunting signals. These are generally rectangular, in contrast to the round block signals, and the two aspects are horizontal rather than vertical. There are also rectangular signals at points and crossovers, which show green for the main line and yellow for the branch, in each case with an arrow superimposed. A red indication is given only when the points are changing. There are also various fixed signals to indicate speed limits etc., and markings by the trackside or on the tunnel walls (a white bar and circle on a dark background) warn of reduced visibility or restricted width.

At certain specially chosen locations in the open air, signal aspects are being renewed using fibre optic lenses. These, although very costly, give greatly improved sighting in conditions of poor visibility.

The maximum speed allowed on the Métro is 70kph (80kph on line 14) but this is only possible where stations are not so close together. Otherwise, the speed allowed is shown by illuminated signs, white on a dark background, and applies from speed restriction to speed restriction, or, if it applies first, the next station. Where the speed may be increased between stations, then this is also shown at the appropriate location.

At terminal stations, the signalling is worked by the local signal cabin, often situated on an over bridge with a view of the station. Here, according to the age of the location, a Chef de Manœuvre may have very modern push-button equipment for operating signals and points, or in days past, an old style lever frame, some of which were akin to 'beer pump handles'. An illuminated diagram of the local area is provided, as well as visual display unit, which shows the position of all trains bound for that terminus on the line, which greatly assists in the forward planning of departure regulation.

At intermediate reversing points along the line, there are two methods of operation. At selected sites, service reversing is performed automatically by the operation of a single switch in the control centre (PCC). The occupation of track circuits and the passage of trains is all that is needed for this system to operate. At other less important emergency reversing points, large levers by the trackside (many of those of a type known as Saxby) require manual intervention and operation, but authority to operate them is given by the control room. This system is also provided at the many interconnections between Métro lines.

Automatic Train Operation

The first experiments on the Métro with Automatic Train Operation (PA or Pilotage Automatique) were carried out from 1951 on the shuttle line (the 'Navette'), concurrently with the experiments with pneumatic tyres on rolling stock. Passengers were carried on the single motor coach most weekday afternoons from 13 April 1952 to 31 May 1956, and the system proved to be totally safe and reliable in operation. However the RATP recognised that there was a difference in testing this system in the quiet backwater of the Navette, and putting it into full operation on a line as busy as line 4. Unfortunately there was not at that time, the finance available to allow a more extensive trial and another decade was to elapse before the idea was revived.

In 1967, line 11 was equipped for ATO and two trains were equipped with the necessary apparatus. Again, there was complete success in operation and all trains were converted by 1969. From then, conversions of the other lines followed, the programme being concluded with line 2 in July 1979. Lines 10, 3bis and 7bis do not have service intervals that are sufficiently short to warrant the expense of conversion to automatic operation and have instead been converted to non-automatic controlled one-person-operation (CMC – Conduite Manuelle Contrôlée).

The system of ATO used on the Métro is based on an induction cable, carrying current drawn from the signalling system and laid between the running rails to the 'Greek pattern'. The cable has a PVC covering and lies on a wooden surface, which is fixed to the sleepers. Messages which are transmitted by the cable are picked up by two collectors placed underneath the middle coach. The cable is divided into two unequal segments, the length of which is determined by the speed of transmission of information and the speed of the train – the average length of time taken to traverse one section is 0.3 seconds. The cable carries two programmes, one for acceleration and one for braking. If a train passes through a section more quickly than it should do, the control equipment activates the brakes until the desired speed is reached. If it is going too slowly, it is made to accelerate. The control equipment itself takes up little space

A view of the tunnel on line 8 under the River Seine between Invalides and Concorde, during track replacement work in April 1994 and before the ATO track equipment was reinstated.
Julian Pepinster

and is housed under one of the seats in the middle coach. In the early applications, it operated on the notches of the controller, but now the process is entirely electronic.

In conjunction with the introduction of the programmed departures from terminal stations (q.v. below), the clock giving the departure time passes on information to the control equipment, which then requests the departure signal from the driver.

In service, ATO has proved to be very reliable. At stations, trains are brought to a halt within 500mm of the desired stopping point.

The ATO equipment on the Métro may be classified into two types, which mainly differ by the frequency band of the electronic signals in between track and machine. Thus, there are the low frequency collecting systems in the 3 to 8kHz range, as used on the earliest converted lines (1, 3 and 4) and the 135kHz collecting systems on lines 2, 5, 6, 7, 8, 9, 11, 12 and 13. The latter system is the most recent and incorporates the latest technological advances, allowing a more flexible operating mode.

Lines were converted to ATO as follows:

September 1967	Line 11	June 1976	Line 8
February 1971	Line 4	April 1977	Line 13
February 1972	Line 1	July 1977	Line 7
July 1973	Line 3	December 1977	Line 12
February 1975	Line 6	April 1978	Line 5
May 1975	Line 9	July 1979	Line 2

When lines were being converted for ATO, the facility for full-speed manual driving was retained, and indeed, it is stipulated that the first train of the day must travel in normal manual mode. Where service intervals are less than two minutes, ATO is obligatory. Service intervals in excess of four minutes demand manual driving. Between the two, the driver has a choice. Originally, ATO was obligatory, except for shunting, but following some shunting mishaps due to driver unfamiliarity, the system just described was introduced.

For those lines not equipped for ATO (10, 3bis and 7bis) and subsequently for manual driving on ATO lines, the system of controlled manual operation was developed for one-person-operated trains. This is the VACMA system (Veille Automatique), which consists of a deadman's pedal and a ring around the controller handle, one of which must be operated every 30 seconds. If a driver omits to do so, an audible warning sounds and an emergency brake application follows. The MF67 and later trains were fitted from new, earlier stock (MP55 and MP59) when modernised. Complementing the VACMA system is CMC (Conduite Manuelle Contrôlée), which generates an alarm should a driver pass a red signal, with the train being brought to a stand. The incident is recorded on the train's tachometer.

All Métro rolling stock has, therefore been equipped for CMC, as follows:

Line	Line Equipped	Stock Equipped	Completion
1	1983–84	1983–85	June 1985
2	1982–84	1981	February 1984
3	1981	1979–80	September 1981
4	1983–85	1982–84	June 1985
5	1983–84	1982–83	April 1985
6	1982–84	1983–83	April 1984
7	1982	1980–81	November 1982
8	1981	1980–81	May 1982
9	1983–84	1982–84	August 1984
10	1974–75	1975–76	1975–76
11	1981	1980–81	August 1981
12	1983	1983	November 1983
13	1980	1979–80	August 1980

The main Métro control centre is located in Boulevard Bourdon, near to Bastille, and comprises two rooms, each having a number of lines. Generally, these lines are arranged in pairs, one above the other, with the two controllers side by side. *RATP*

Train Service Control

In former times, when Métro operated with short trains and short interstation distances, the frequency of trains was comparatively low. However, as traffic has risen, it has been necessary to increase frequencies during busy times, and service regularity has become increasingly sensitive to even slight disturbances.

At the start it was incumbent on the supervising staff distributed over the lines to take appropriate corrective measures in the event of breakdowns. This often led to long, random and imprecise service intervals. Before the advent of the central control room, heavy rush hour traffic and subsequent extended station stops generated late running of the services. On line 1, for example, the accumulated late running in the peaks under normal conditions was 22 minutes.

To enable more efficient control of trains, therefore, the RATP has, over a period of time, linked its Métro lines to a central control, or PCC (Poste de Commande Centralisée), where all operations are monitored. Rapid communications are provided in the form of telephone links to key locations, and a two-way high-frequency carrier wave radio between drivers and the PCC. An illuminated diagram for each line is provided, arranged in pairs, one above the other, where train movement can be observed by train numbers and track circuit occupation. In the event of a service disruption, the controllers have every facility to deal with the situation. This may vary from spacing out trains to allow equal but maximum loading, to reversing the service short of a breakdown and operating an emergency timetable. Each diagram has facilities to charge or discharge traction current, or to divide a section. Other facilities provided include signal telephone communications, control of the remaining portillon gates at platform entrances (the high service reliability of recent years, through central control, ATO, programmed departures and reduced station stop times, has made these almost unnecessary), and direct communication with station ticket offices. Although

Because line 14 (Météor) is a totally automatic railway, its control centre has been purpose-built on the line at Bercy, rather than being an add-on to the conventional system at Boulevard Bourdon. All functions related to a completely automatic railway are dealt with in the new control room, which includes supervising train movements without train crews, and interior train monitoring. *RATP*

service regulation is carried out by computer, it is possible for manual intervention by the PCC. In either case, a train being held for regulation is indicated to the driver by three flashing white lights in a triangular shape, located adjacent to the station starting signal.

The PCC is located in Boulevard Bourdon, almost diagonally opposite to the entrance to the closed station of Arsenal on line 5. It is within short walking distance of Bastille (lines 1, 5 and 8), Quai de la Rapée (5) and Sully Morland (7). The first line to be connected to PCC operation was line 1 on 15 June 1967, and immediately the peak accumulated late running on that line diminished from 22 minutes to just 2.5 minutes. Other lines were subsequently linked to PCC operation, the last being achieved in 1975. Dates were as follows:

June 1967	Line 1	May 1973	Line 2
September 1967	Line 11	June 1973	Line 5
February 1969	Line 4	July 1974	Line 13
March 1969	Line 7	July 1974	Line 14*
February 1970	Lines 3/3bis	September 1974	Line 10
October 1970	Line 9	November 1974	Line 6
May 1971	Line 8	February 1975	Line 7bis
September 1971	Line 12		

Note * Merged with line 13 on 9 November 1976.

The PCC actually comprises two large circular rooms, interconnected, one with lines 2, 5, 6, 11 and 13, the other containing lines 1, 3/3bis, 4, 7/7bis, 8, 9 and 12. The new line 14 (Météor) has its own control room at Bercy.

Programmed departures

Around 30 years ago, the minimum headways during peak hours were not less than 1min 50sec. In order to reduce these minimum headways on which the carrying capacity of the Métro depends, the RATP came up with the operating principle known as 'Programmed Departures' from terminal stations. Under this system the operating instructions are displayed along successive stations, on a digital clock face telling drivers of each train the 'staggered terminal departure time'. This is the actual time (expressed only in minutes and seconds), less the theoretical travel time between the departure terminal and the considered station. Thus, to follow the timetable, the driver has to leave the station when the time coincides with the terminal departure time. For example, with a train that leaves the terminal at, say 08.05.15, the driver should depart from the stations along the route when the clock displays '05.15'. Each clock also gives the type of running schedule then in operation, which differs during the course of the day. There are four different running times – Heaviest flow peak (marche 'A'), counterflow peak ('B'), midday off-peak ('C'), and evening off-peak ('D').

Drivers are kept advised of the permissible dwell time in stations by means of a buzzer, triggered by computer or manually from the PCC. The driver then activates the door closing button which, in turn, activates a pleasant audible sound over the doors, warning passengers of the imminent closing of the doors by a second push on the same button. When a train arrives at a station with a delay exceeding a given threshold, the sound warning by the buzzer is given a few seconds in advance of the permissible dwell time to enable the train to absorb its delay a little at a time.

The programmed departures system, first put into use on line 7 in 1969, is now operative on all lines except 10, 11, 3bis and 7bis. By this means, it has been possible to increase the number of trains by shortening the headways (to as little as 1min 35sec), thus raising the line capacity by 15–20%, without changing the signalling system.

The south end of the southbound platform at Place d'Italie on line 7, showing the CCTV monitors and the four different schedules (A, B, C and D), which relate to the relevant time of day. Note that above the TV monitors indications are given as to which part of the train is covered by the picture. *Brian Hardy*

Timetables

Train services on the Métro are timetabled to a precision of five seconds. There are three different services provided within the seven-day week: Mondays to Fridays, Saturdays and Sundays. Within theses different types of schedules, there are several service level variations, which can be summarised as follows:

On Mondays to Fridays, there are four schedules operated throughout the year. The full service timetable operates from October to April. During May, June and September, a slightly reduced service is provided on most lines, followed by a further reduction for the month of July. The fourth and lowest level of service applies during the month of August, when many Parisians leave the capital for their annual holiday. The first reduction service also applies on most lines on Mondays to Fridays during the Christmas and Easter school holidays. Until recently, it was the practice that fewer trains operated in the morning peak because of the protracted nature of the morning rush period. In the evening peak, however, where the busy period was more concentrated, the maximum service was operated. More recently, with extended shopping hours, lines 4, 6, 11 and 13 have a similar morning and evening peak.

As an example, the four different service levels for line 1 are as follows – the figures show the number of trains in service for each period and the scheduled service interval:

Monday to Friday	Morning Peak		Midday		Evening Peak		Evening	
Full Service	42	1'55"	25	3'25"	46	1'50"	11	7'50"
First reduction	42	1'55"	24	3'35"	42	2'00"	11	7'50"
July	32	2'35"	23	3'50"	35	2'25"	11	7'50"
August	27	3'15"	19	4'40"	31	2'50"	11	7'50"

Saturday	08.00 to 09.00		Morning		Afternoon Busy		Evening	
Winter Service	19	4'25"	20	4'25"	26	3'20"	11	7'50"
Summer Service	18	4'55"	18	4'55"	20	4'20"	11	7'50"

Sunday	05.30 to 06.30		Morning		Afternoon Busy		Evening	
Winter Service	12	7'15"	16	5'35"	22	4'00"	11	7'50"
Summer Service	12	7'15"	15	5'50"	19	4'35"	11	7'50"

The Paris Métro operates from 05.30 daily, when the first trains depart from the terminal stations. At some former terminal stations, for example, on line 9 at 05.30, trains start from the two termini (Pont de Sèvres and Mairie de Montreuil) as well as from République (both directions), Porte de Saint-Cloud (going east) and Porte de Montreuil (going west). At night, the last trains arrive at the terminal stations at 01.15. Because of the short distances between stations, the complex network of lines, and various interchange corridors, there are no last train connections between the various Métro lines. In common with other European systems, the Paris Métro is a 365-day-a-year underground railway network – even a good service is provided on Christmas Day with the operation of Sunday schedules from the usual 05.30 to 01.15. The UK public transport operators still seem to be something of an exception at Christmas time!

Since the previous edition of this book, all trains on line 8 now work through to Créteil Préfecture, Maisons-Alfort Les Juilliottes no longer being used for short-working services apart from trains entering or leaving service there. A similar situation also applied on line 10 from October 1994, with all trains operating to and from Boulogne. Porte d'Auteuil therefore ceased to be an intermediate terminus apart from the trains starting or stabling there and since the autumn of 1997, no trains are scheduled to terminate there, apart from the last two service trains of the day.

The most frequent peak service remains on line 4, every 1min 40sec, an honour now shared with line 7 between La Courneuve and Maison Blanche.

Track

The rails used on the Métro have always been highly standardised. Vignoles rail of a weight of 52kg/m was used on line 1 when it was built. These rails were 15 metres long, but when line 2 was constructed, rails 18 metres long were used and this length has remained the standard ever since. The rails are laid on sleepers at the rate of one sleeper every 750mm. They are fastened down with sleeper screws and are joined together with fishplates. The track is embedded in a ballast of crushed stone. On recent extensions, a concrete trackbed with rubber inserts has been used. This latter type of construction is thought to absorb vibration more readily than the traditional permanent way and, as less attention needs to be paid to levelling, it is easier and quicker to install.

The Nord-Sud had a more individual elastic approach, probably adopted because of the sharp curvature of line 12. It used bullhead rails, slightly deeper than those of the CMP (165mm as against 150mm) which were supported by chairs incorporating a cushion of linoleum and fixed to the sleepers with a cork insert. The sleepers on the Nord-Sud were spaced at a greater distance apart than on the CMP – 1.40m as against 750mm. Unfortunately the linoleum and cork inserts soon lost their elasticity and disintegrated, causing vertical movements in the track and severe corrugation. Such track had a short life and was quickly replaced by standard construction after the merger with the CMP in 1930, although a small length of the original track can still be observed on the third track at Porte de Versailles station.

Welding of running rails was not adopted until 1960, since traditional methods allowed for speedy replacement. However, welding was adopted when line 1 was converted to 'pneu' operation and its advantages were such that it was soon adopted for all lines and by 1980 most track was of welded construction. Only at curves and crossings and on the elevated sections of lines 2 and 6 are traditional methods still used, in the latter case to avoid placing undue stress on the pillars of the viaducts. Rails on curves generally have to be replaced every three years, but elsewhere they normally have a life of 15–20 years.

Because of the normal end-to-end method of operation of most Métro lines, the number of points and crossovers, apart from terminal areas, is relatively limited. Only lines 7, 10 and 13 have junctions (at Maison Blanche, Auteuil and La Fourche respectively), but all of these are arranged to avoid the crossing of lines on the flat, a 'flying junction' arrangement being constructed to avoid service delays caused by 'flat' junctions. Many points are normally fixed in the straight position, and often facing points instead of trailing points are used. Points at terminal stations have been electrically controlled since 1911, and many crossovers on the line of route have been similarly equipped since the PCC system of control was introduced from 1967. There remains however, a number of hand-worked points at locations considered as less important, and at some of the interline connections. Authority for the use of these points is given by the PCC, although it is necessary for a member of the line staff to be present if used in passenger traffic hours when the points are unprotected by a signal.

The third rail was originally bullhead of 38kg/m but this was very quickly changed to a much heavier Vignoles rail, then again to the present 'T' section rail of 52kg/m. It is placed at a distance of 330mm from the running rail and is fixed by means of plastic-type insulators to every fourth sleeper. Traction current returns via the running rails, which have to be bonded. It should be noted that the actual track gauge of the Métro is fractionally wider than standard, at 1.44m. In contrast, the spacing between the tracks is only 1.33m, as opposed to main line railways standard of 1.85m.

The track used by the rubber-tyred 'pneu' trains consists of two broad 'I' beams of metal, each 300mm wide, placed outside the normal running rails, at a distance from centre to centre of 1.98m. On line 11, much of the original 'pneu' trackwork was originally of tropical hardwood, but this was replaced during track renewal in 1982–83. Reinforced concrete surfaces are sometimes used in stations and, on the elevated sections of line 6, they are ribbed to improve adhesion in wet or frosty weather. Outside

The only gated level crossing on the Métro network is on the non-passenger section between Nation and Charonne depot on line 2, where it crosses the Rue de Lagny at the depot entrance. A train on line 2 is seen on the level crossing. *John Herting*

the 'I' beams, two lateral bars support the horizontal guide wheels, which also serve as the positive current rails. The ordinary running rails are retained throughout. If a tyre should lose pressure in service (which is a very unusual occurrence) then the train will automatically switch to the use of these rails. The conventional running rails also act for current return and shoes from the train make continuous contact with them, hence them remaining in shiny condition. Conventional rolling stock can therefore operate on the 'pneu' lines, but a special lateral current collector shoe has to be fitted.

Electricity Supply and Distribution
During the first half of this century, electricity production was by different private companies. The Métro had first tried to produce its own electricity, but quite unsuccessfully.

The power station at Bercy was not ready for use in 1900 and, when work finally resumed, it was not powerful enough to serve a quickly-growing Métro system. It thus served from 1901 to 1927, producing a fraction of the total current consumed. The system was damaged in the great flood of 1910 and final abandonment came when 25Hz a.c. production ended. The Métro therefore took most of its electricity from private companies, which were in fact part of Baron Empain's financial empire, as was the CMP!

Electric power supplied for Métro operation was provided in the form of high voltage alternating current from three Métro plants and two Electricité de France (EDF) substations located at Saint-Denis, Ivry, Billancourt, Vitry Nord and Arcueil. Three-phase 10,000 volt cables led from EDF plants to various substations, where the power was stepped down and converted into 600V d.c. for the Métro, and to 1,500V dc for the Ligne de Sceaux (now RER line B). High voltage cubicles, many of which were located in the substations, make up the grid of the power system.

The transformation of electrical supplies took place between 1958 and 1970, with a system enlargement in 1978–79. This enabled control of ancillary equipment and facilities, such as station lighting, modern ticketing and computer equipment by the RATP for the first time. High voltage supplied by the EDF from the 63kV grid in the Greater Paris region, to four stations at Monttessuy, Père Lachaise A and B, Lamarck and Denfert, was distributed throughout Paris and from the 225kV grid to further stations at Père Lachaise C, Rene Coty A and B and Ney. All these high-voltage stations step down to 15,000 volts for distribution to 138 rectifier substations equipped with medium voltage silicon rectifiers (1,750 to 4,500kW). In addition, given the distance from the high voltage RATP stations, 19 rectifier substations are directly fed from the EDF at 20kV.

The rectifier substations feed the 750 volt and 1,500 volt traction current supplies, so spaced that any one of them can be shut down without detriment, the other surrounding rectifier substations supplying the required replacement power due to their diversity. In each rectifier substation the equipment making up the substation is separated into readily removable, interchangeable and transportable units. Each unit is of standard modules so that in the event of a breakdown, it is possible to replace the defective equipment without delay, by means of specially equipped breakdown vehicles. Power is also distributed to 523 stepdown transformer units (15kW/380–220 volts) feeding power to the electrical installations in tunnels and at stations, as well as to sundry administrative buildings, bus garages and workshops.

The station lighting circuits are fed from transformer substations located in 'power and lighting stations' (PEF – Poste Éclairage Force). For reasons of security there are two entirely separate sources of supply. In the event of failure of the overall RATP power system, standby electric generating sets are remote controlled from the Electrical Control Room (PCE – which actually adjoins the Métro PCC), which clusters together all of the high voltage station controls.

Substations on the Métro are generally about 3km apart. For ease of identification in the PCC, current stations are named and numbered. If current is required off for any reason, then the tracks in both directions will be isolated. On the main running lines, it is not possible to isolate just one track, although there is a facility to divide a section to enable an emergency crossover to be used, should it be in the current section with the problem, but away from the actual problem itself. On the other hand, extensive isolation facilities exist at terminal stations, where there are often a number of stabling sidings. Facilities exist on every Métro platform for passengers to discharge traction current. These are contained in a cabinet which has other passenger aids (such as communication with the station supervisor and a fire extinguisher) and are protected by a glass screen: a pull-ring automatically cuts off the current. These pull-rings are also located in tunnels, spaced at 50 metre intervals.

At night, current is only taken off on the Métro when work in tunnels or on the track is scheduled. The system must therefore be regarded as 'live' at all times.

Tunnels

Generally in Paris, Métro tunnels have been made as shallow as possible. Only on lines constructed later did these go to any great depth and this was for the reason of passing under existing lines when they were crossed. New extensions into the suburbs are also built just below the surface.

Some of the Métro was originally built by the 'cut and cover' method, such stations being recognised by their girder roofs. Almost all of the tunnel extensions from the 1970s have been built by this method, where a trench is dug out, the route constructed, and then covered over again. However, much of the original Métro was constructed by the 'Belgian Method'. In this method, a pilot gallery is cut following the line of the upper part of the main tunnel. Shafts are dug to this at intervals for the removal of the spoil. From this gallery, by digging sideways and supporting the earth above by props and wooden planks, space is obtained for building the roof of the tunnel with masonry. Under this roof the gallery can be widened into a covered trench along the line of the tunnel. From this trench every few metres, side trenches are dug to where the walls are to be built. The walls, also of masonry, are built under the roof, giving a masonry arch tunnel, of 'basket handle' cross section, resting on concrete footings The whole of the tunnel cross-section is then excavated. The tunnel floor, or invert, of concrete is next added. The invert is slightly curved in dry ground, or more curved if water is present, in which case it is also waterproofed. Finally, liquid cement is injected behind the masonry work of the tunnel, to fill any voids left by the compression of the soil.

The connection between line 10 at Cluny La Sorbonne and line 4 at Odéon. The centre track at the former station leads down and underneath line 10, which is seen at the top of the picture. This view is taken on 15 May 1996. *Julian Pepinster*

In the early days, it was thought that technology was insufficiently advanced to tunnel under the River Seine and, for that reason, the original lines were built to cross over it on a viaduct. These were arranged as follows:

Original line	Present line	Between
2-Sud	6	Passy – Bir-Hakeim
5	5	Gare d'Austerlitz – Quai de La Rapée
6	6	Quai de La Gare – Bercy

In addition, line 1 was built to cross over the Saint-Martin canal at Bastille.

However, the decision was subsequently taken to construct future Métro lines under the river, although the various schemes were not without difficulties. To that end, however, the following crossings were made in tunnel:

- Line 4 between Châtelet and Cité, and between Cité and Saint Michel, both in a double track tunnel formed of a sunken caisson in a trench in the river bed (opened in 1910).
- Line 10 between Javel and Mirabeau, constructed as line 4 (opened in 1913).
- Line 8 between Concorde and Invalides is similarly constructed (opened 1913).
- Line 7 between Sully – Morland and Jussieu is in a double-track shield-driven tube, of cast iron segments, 7.25m internal diameter (opened 1931).
- Line 12, between Concorde and Assemblée Nationale, is in two single track shield-driven tubes of 5m diameter, and is thus unique to the Métro (opened 1910).

Under-river sections constructed in recent times are:

- Line 13 between Invalides and Champs-Élysées – Clemenceau (opened 1976).
- Line 14 between Cour Saint-Émilion and Bibliothèque (opened 1998).

Other above river crossings made in the open include line 8 over the River Marne between Charenton-Écoles and École Vétériniare de Maisons-Alfort (opened in 1970) and on line 1 over the River Seine between Pont de Neuilly and Esplanade de La Défense (opened 1992). To tunnel under the River Seine on the latter extension was originally planned (and to that end a large area under the La Défense development lies abandoned today) and would have created an impossibly steep gradient between Esplanade de La Défense and the climb up to La Défense, and problems in the siting of a much-needed station at the former.

The connection between lines 1 and 2 at Étoile became disused in 1935 when the depot at Fontenay opened and trains on line 1 became maintained there instead of at Charonne. Although the points leading to the connection were removed, the track within remained, as seen in this June 1991 view. *Julian Pepinster*

A small maintenance workshop was provided underground at Mairie des Lilas when line 11 opened in 1937 and was upgraded in the mid-1950s to maintain the then new rubber tyred trains. In this 1992 view a train of MP55 stock is on the left and a train of MP73 stock on the right. In the background can be seen a depot works motor car (TA). *RATP*

Depots and Stabling Points

A feature of the Paris Métro rolling stock depots is that they are used only for train maintenance and not for stabling trains during slack periods or at weekends. Trains not required for maintenance are stabled 'on the line' at numerous positions, generally at terminal stations. Each line of the Métro has a depot for routine maintenance, and some of these have been specially adapted for repairs and major overhauls. The depots and their locations can be summarised as follows:

Line 1   FONTENAY (east of terminus Chateau de Vincennes), opened in 1934. It was heavily rebuilt in 1996–98 to accommodate the MP89 stock on both lines 1 and 14. This depot also has access to the SNCF main line, through the disused goods depot at Fontenay-sous-Bois and RER line A.

Line 2   CHARONNE (east of Nation) was the first maintenance depot for the Métro. This served lines 1 and 2, the former until 1934, when Fontenay depot opened and took over maintenance on line 1. Access to the main line via the Petite Ceinture was provided in the form of a 15% grade ramp, which was abolished after a connection became available at Fontenay. Charonne depot was rebuilt in the 1980s to accommodate modern rolling stock. Access to line 2 from the depot is by crossing the Rue de Lagny, the only operational level crossing on the Métro system, albeit on a non-passenger section of line.

Line 3   SAINT-FARGEAU (east of Gambetta), opened in December 1904. The metal structure of this building has achieved 'listed' status.

Line 4   SAINT-OUEN (north of Porte de Clignancourt), opened in April 1908.

The depot for line 10 is also underground – near to Porte d'Auteuil. This view shows the last train of MA51 stock (left), which last ran in service in June 1994, before the transfer of unit E023 for preservation and the scrapping of E034. On the right is a train of MF67E stock. *Julian Pepinster*

Line 5	BOBIGNY (between the two Bobigny stations) was opened April 1988, although extensive stabling sidings were provided from the opening of the Bobigny extension in 1985. The depot also maintains the trams for route T1 between Bobigny and Saint-Denis.
Line 6	PLACE D'ITALIE, opened in April 1906.
Line 7	CHOISY (access from Porte de Choisy) opened in 1931 and took over the maintenance of trains on line 7 from Villette (q.v. below).
Line 7bis	PRÉ-SAINT-GERVAIS, opened in 1994. This one-track depot has been for routine maintenance of the small fleet of MF88 trains on line 7bis, occupying the former shuttle platform, which is now separated from the single platform for passengers. Heavier maintenance is done at Saint-Fargeau.
Line 8	JAVEL (access from Lourmel) opened in 1937.
Line 9	BOULOGNE (access from Pont de Sèvres) opened in 1934.
Line 10	PORTE D'AUTEUIL opened with line 8 in 1913 and also maintained trains on line 9 on its opening from 1922 until Boulogne depot opened 12 years later.
Line 11	MAIRIE DES LILAS (east of station) was opened in 1937. It was modernised in 1956 to accommodate the (first generation) rubber-tyred trains of MP55 stock.
Line 12	VAUGIRARD (access from Porte de Versailles) opened in 1910. This depot also has access to the main line via the Petit Ceinture via a hand-signalled road crossing of the Rue Desnouettes.

Line 13   PLEYEL (access from Carrefour Pleyel) opened in 1968.

Line 13   BAGNEUX, south of Châtillon – Montrouge, was opened in September 1998, as an additional workshop for the ever expanding line 13.

Line 14   TOLBIAC – NATIONALE became available in 1996 during the construction of Météor. The depot is in fact at the site of the future station Olympiades, which is due to open in 2005, by which time, the depot would have moved to the next station on the line of route, at Maison Blanche. It comprises two tracks with pit roads and washing facilities on each.

In addition, the depot for engineers' trains is located at VILLETTE, near Porte de la Villette at the northern part of line 7, with maintenance of engineers' vehicles being undertaken at Vaugirard depot. Villette depot was originally responsible for the rolling stock on line 7 until Choisy depot opened in 1931.

Three of the above depots are in fact located underground, these being Pré-Saint-Gervais, Porte d'Auteuil and Mairie des Lilas. Two other depots, Javel and Playel, are roofed over. All of the maintenance depots have inspection pits. Most also have lifting facilities and some have travelling cranes to move equipment around the depot area. Four of the depots have been adapted to perform major overhauls. These are at Fontenay (which deals with all the 'pneu' stock), Choisy (the first generation of modern steel-wheel-on-steel-rail trains – the MF67), Saint-Ouen (the latest of modern stock – the MF77) and Vauguard (for engineers' trains and a small percentage of the MF67 stock). During heavy overhaul, the cars are lifted to allow disassembly and inspection of the major components, such as axles, traction motors, bogies and compressors. There are specialised areas dealing with axle and bogie frame refurbishing, sheet metal work and welding, battery servicing and seat covering repairs. Motor cars undergo a major overhaul at 400,000km intervals, while trailers are overhauled every 500,000km. Painting of the car bodies is not always done to correspond with overhauls and like many other European transport operators, the RATP has had to contend with the menace of graffiti.

The open-air sidings at Bobigny on line 5. A stranger in the camp seen on 13 January 1999 is the three-car train of MF88 stock which operates on line 7bis. *Brian Hardy*

Returning now to trains stabled 'on the line', each terminal area has a number of specified locations where it is possible to stable trains. Crews are informed of the train's location by referring to a green chalkboard or white board, which is updated by the terminal station supervisor. Trains are generally identified on these boards by the centre car, and in the train formations they are usually arranged in numerical order of these cars. On the leading cabs of all trains, a two- or three-digit 'set number' in large white letters indicates the number of the centre car. Identification of the stabling location is by numbers and letters, and in places which have more than one arrival or departure platform, these are often used to stable trains during the day. Often a serviceable spare train is kept ready to changeover any train that may become defective and will require replacement in service.

The following table lists the maximum number of trains required for service on each line:

Line 1			*Line 8*	
La Défense	4		Balard	10
Porte Maillot	12		Lourmel	6
Château de Vincennes	30		République	4
	46		Maisons-Alfort – les Juilliottes	12
Line 2			Créteil-Préfecture	19
Porte Dauphine	6			51
Nation	33			
	39		*Line 9*	
			Pont de Sèvres	10
Line 3			Porte de Saint-Cloud	25
Gallieni	12		République	2
Porte des Lilas (3bis)	12		Porte de Montreuil	7
Porte de Champerret	11		Mairie de Montreuil	15
Pont de Levallois	5			59
	40			
			Line 10	
Line 3bis			Gare d'Austerlitz	8
Porte des Lilas	4		Porte d'Auteuil	14
	4			22
Line 4				
Porte de Clignancourt	27		*Line 11*	
Porte d'Orléans	15		Châtelet	8
	42		Porte des Lilas	6
			Mairie des Lilas	4
Line 5				18
Bobigny	31			
Église de Pantin	5		*Line 12*	
Place d'Italie	9		Porte de la Chapelle	11
	45		Porte de Versailles	11
Line 6			Mairie d'Issy	12
Nation	15			34
Place d'Italie	6			
Kléber	16		Line 13	
	37		Gabriel Péri	7
			Porte de Clichy	3
Line 7			Saint-Denis – Université	5
La Courneuve	12		Carrefour Pleyel	6
Porte de La Villette	20		Invalides	10
Porte d'Ivry	9		Châtillon – Montrouge	19
Mairie d'Ivry	10			50
Villejuif – Louis Aragon	13			
	64		*Line 14*	
			Madeleine	5
Line 7bis			Bibliothèque	8
Pré-Saint-Gervais	6			13
	6			

There are, in addition, a number of stabling sidings around the Métro system, as listed below, although some of them are used for stabling engineers' trains:

Line 1	*Line 2*	*Line 3*
Porte Maillot	Blanche	Arts et Métiers
	Belleville	

Line 4	*Line 5*	*Line 6*
Etienne Marcel	République	Bercy
Saint-Germain des Prés		Edgar Quinet

Line 7	*Line 9*	*Line 12*
Cade	Alma Marceau	Trinité
Pont Neuf		Montparnasse-Bienvenüe

Former terminal stations continue to have stabling areas for trains as follows:

Line 5	*Line 8*	*Line 13*
Porte de Pantin	Charenton – Écoles	Porte de Saint-Ouen
	Porte de Charenton	Porte de Vanves

SUMMARY OF TRAIN SERVICE INTERVALS

Line	No. of Daily Deps	Section	Morning peak		Midday		Evening peak		Evening	
1	359	Château de Vincennes to Grande Arche de La Défense	42	1'55"	25	3'25"	46	1'50"	11	7'50"
2	344	Nation to Porte Dauphine	35	2'00"	22	3'20"	39	1'50"	9	8'15"
3	361	Porte de Champerret to Gallieni	36	1'55"	21	3'30"	40	1'45"	9	8'30"
3bis	259	Porte des Lilas to Gambetta	4	3'15"	3	4'15"	4	3'00"	2	8'30"
4	420	Porte de Clignancourt to Porte d'Orleans	40	1'40"	23	3'00"	42	1'40"	10	7'00"
5	358	Place d'Italie to Bobigny	40	1'50"	24	3'20"	45	1'45"	10	8'15"
6	336	Charles de Gaulle – Étoile to Nation	37	1'55"	20	3'45"	37	1'55"	10	7'30"
7	384	La Courneuve to Maison Blanche	60	1'45"	32	3'30"	64	1'40"	19	6'00"
		Maison Blanche to Villejuif		3'30"		7'00"		3'20"		12'00"
		Maison Blanche to Mairie d'Ivry		3'30"		7'00"		3'20"		12'00"
7bis	215	Louis Blanc to Pré-Saint-Gervais	6	4'10"	5	5'00"	6	4'10"	3	8'45"
8	310	Balard to Créteil Préfecture	45	2'30"	30	3'55"	51	2'10"	14	8'30"
9	363	Mairie de Montreuil to Pont de Sèvres	56	1'50"	32	3'35"	59	1'45"	16	7'30"
10	258	Gare d'Austerlitz to Boulogne	21	3'10"	16	4'10"	22	3'00"	8	8'30"
11	354	Châtelet to Mairie des Lilas	18	2'00"	10	3'55"	18	2'05"	5	7'45"
12	305	Porte de La Chapelle to Mairie d'Issy	32	2'35"	24	3'30"	34	2'20"	12	7'00"
13	408	Châtillon Montrouge to La Fourche	50	1'45"	25	3'35"	50	1'45"	14	6'00"
		La Fourche to Gabriel Péri		5'15"		7'10"		†		12'00"
		La Fourche to Saint-Denis		*		7'10"		†		12'00"
14	450	Madeleine to Bibliothèque	13	2'00"	12	2'30"	13	2'00"	6	4'30"

Notes:
* Saint-Denis is served by two trains every 5'15".
† Evening peak service pattern to northern branches is in groups of five trains every 8'45" in the sequence Gabriel Péri/Saint-Denis/Gabriel Péri/Saint-Denis/Saint-Denis.

Terminal Stations

Even from the very beginnings of the Métro, the facilities provided at terminal stations were variable. Now, with 14 main lines and two branches, there is even greater variety, which provides much operational interest to the student of underground railways:

1. Reversing Beyond Station

Here, there are separate arrival and departing platforms and trains reversing have to proceed to a shunting neck, at which there is a narrow platform walkway (called a 'trottoir') for drivers to change ends. In quiet periods, it is possible for the train operator to change ends and take the train on its next journey. During peak periods, a number of shunting operators may be available to speed up operations – necessary when service intervals as frequent as 1min 40sec are being worked.

There are several variations to this method of working at terminal stations. The arrival platform may be served by two tracks, in which case trains may be accepted at intervals which are nearly as short as the time required to empty a train in peak hours. On the other hand , if the departure platform has two tracks (and there are instances where terminal stations have two tracks on arrival and departure), then the interval between the departing trains may be shortened, or a spare train may be kept at one platform, ready to leave to fill a gap in the service caused by late running, or to replace a failed train. One track at the terminal station usually has an inspection pit, to allow maintenance staff to examine trains.

The above arrangements apply to: Château de Vincennes and La Défense (line 1), Gallieni* and Pont de Levallois (line 3), Bobigny-Pablo Picasso† and Place d'Italie (line 5), La Courneuve†, Mairie d'Ivry and Villejuif-Louis Aragon* (line 7), Balard† and Créteil – Préfecture† (line 8), Pont de Sèvres† and Mairie de Montreuil (line 9), Gare d'Austerlitz (line 10), Châtelet and Mairie des Lilas* (line 11), Porte de la Chapelle† and Mairie d'Issy (line 12), Châtillon Montrouge†, Saint-Denis – Université* and Gabriel Péri (line 13).

At locations marked (*), it is possible for trains to run direct into the departure platform under signals, or into a middle platform (†), to speed up turn around time during service difficulties, or during certain off-peak periods of operation.

One other station with shunting arrangements, but of an unusual nature, is at Louis Blanc on line 7bis, which offers cross platform interchange with services on line 7. In fact the station comprises two separate sections – southbound on top of northbound. Trains from Pré-Saint-Gervais enter the southbound platform and a shunt operator takes the train out empty once passengers have alighted, clear of the points which then lead to the northbound, into which platform the incoming operator brings the train.

On line 14 the trains reverse (automatically) beyond both terminal stations.

2. Non-Passenger Loops

With this arrangement, trains detrain in the arrival platform and then proceed empty via a loop to the departure platform. This eliminates the need for drivers to change ends and allows scheduled departures at as little as 1 min 35 sec intervals to be operated, a feature that was common to line 4 until a short while ago. This peak hour interval has now been reduced to 1min 40sec on what is still the busiest line of the Métro. According to the location, it is sometimes possible for a number of trains to be in the loop at the same time and facilitates the regulation of the service, as the interval between planned and possible departure times can be observed and adjusted as necessary.

Locations with this arrangement comprise Porte Dauphine* (line 2), Porte des Lilas*† (line 3bis), Porte de Clignancourt and Porte d'Orleans*† (line 4).

At locations marked (*) it is possible to run direct into the departure platform under signals, while at terminal stations marked (†) there is also a 'trottoir' provided, which can be used to reverse trains as an alternative to the loop.

3. Passenger Loops

These are perhaps the most interesting of the terminal station arrangements, as far as the enthusiast is concerned, with the warren of tunnels and sidings, and trains weaving in between stabled trains. These exist at Nation (line 2), Charles de Gaulle-Étoile and Nation (line 6), Pré-Saint-Gervais (line 7bis) and Porte d'Auteuil (line 10). Unlike the two previous operations described above, the passenger loops often aggravate any irregularities in the service.

Interesting operating alternatives are available at the two loops on line 6. At Charles de Gaulle-Étoile, with only one track at the station, separate arrival and departure platforms are provided. However, due to the restricted nature of this arrangement, trains do not take their layover times here – this is done at the next station in the southbound direction, at Kléber, which has two island platforms, one for each direction. It is also possible for a train to reverse at Étoile and travel back on the northbound line, gaining its correct track at Kléber.

The loop at Nation on line 6 is in fact only used in the peaks by departing trains. At other times, when trains are stabled in this loop, reversing service trains can either proceed forward to the 'trottoir', or reverse at one side of the terminal island platforms.

4. Dead End Terminal Stations

There are only two terminal stations on the Métro which do not have tracks going beyond the platforms, in either sidings or loops. These are at Gambetta (line 3bis) and Boulogne – Pont de Saint-Cloud (line 10), both being island platforms with a track each side. At the former location, this platform was originally used by trains on line 3 proceeding to central Paris, cut short when branch line 3bis was created in 1971 so that main line 3 could serve new platforms at Gambetta and the then newly built extension to Gallieni. The present connecting subway between the line 3bis platforms and the new Gambetta station on line 3 (central Paris direction) uses the tunnel formerly occupied by the Métro.

The sharp non-passenger loop on line 2 at Porte Dauphine is seen with a train of MF67E stock in the new RATP colours of jade green and white. *RATP*

Interline Connections

The number of non-passenger connections between Métro lines is numerous and no one Métro line is totally isolated, even though a number of connections may have to be used to reach the ultimate destination. The most frequent use of the connections is made by works trains at night, most of which start their journey in the small hours from the depot near Porte de la Villette on line 7, after the last south bound train has departed at 00.35. The connections are also used, but to a lesser extent, by stock transfers between lines and for overhaul and maintenance.

The length of the connections, of course, varies with the location, but can be as long as 1.83km between lines 9 and 10 from Porte de Saint-Cloud to Auteuil via the never opened station of Porte Molitor, or as short as the length of a pair of points, such as between lines 5 and 7 side by side at Gare de l'Est. However, a buffer now separates lines 9 and 10 and it is no longer possible to go directly from one line to another by this route, nor via Auteuil depot. The various line connections are as follows:

Lines	At/Between
1–2	Charles de Gaulle – Étoille (closed and points lifted)
1–6	Charles de Gaulle – Étoille
1–8	Champs-Élysées – Clemenceau (1) and Concorde (8)
1–5	Gare de Lyon (1) and Quai de la Rapée (5)
1–2	Nation
1–6	Nation
2–4–5	Anvers (2) and Gare du Nord (4 and 5)
2–3	Père-Lachaise
2–9	Nation
3–7	Opéra
3–11	Arts et Métiers
3–5	République
3–3b	Gambetta
3b–7b*	Porte des Lilas (3b) and Place des Fêtes (7b)
3b–7b‡	Porte des Lilas (3b) and Pré-Saint-Gervais (7b)
4–10	Odéon (4) and Cluny La Sorbonne (10)
4–12	Vavin (4) and Montparnasse-Bienvenüe (12)
4–6	Vavin (4) and Edgar Quinet (6)
5–6	Place d'Italie
5–7	Place d'Italie
6–7	Place d'Italie
5–7	Gare de l'Est
5–8	République
6–8	Daumesnil
6–9†	Trocadéro
6–14	Bercy
7–10	Place Monge (7) and Maubert-Mutualité (10)
7–7b†	Louis Blanc
8–9†	République
8–10	La Motte-Picquet – Grenelle
8–13*	Invalides
9–10‡	Porte de Saint-Cloud (9) and Auteuil (10)
9–10	Porte de Saint-Cloud (9) and Porte Molitor
9–10	Michel-Ange-Auteuil
10–13	Duroc (closed and track/points lifted)
12–13	Montparnasse-Bienvenüe
12–13	Saint-Lazare

* Used for stabling trains   † Two separate connections, one in each direction.
‡ Used for stabling trains – through running impossible now.

The New Image of the RATP

Neither the CMP nor the RATP made much effort to develop a house style for use on posters or in publicity material. However, in 1981 a solution, brilliant in its simplicity, was conceived. The brand image would be the ticket, the ordinary yellow and brown Métro and bus ticket. But as successful as 'Le Ticket' was in terms of visual identity, the RATP wanted to create a totally new visual identity to coincide with a new image. To that end, the new image and new company logo were launched in January 1992. The logo comprises a green circle, representing a 'green' Paris, which is cut by a blue line representing the River Seine, but in the shape of a human face, looking upwards towards the future, and portrays the RATP's new image of being more welcoming and human. Very quickly the new logo became widely used throughout the RATP, on documentation and publicity, and from 21 March 1992, the familiar yellow tickets were ousted by the new 'green' tickets bearing the new logo.

A more gradual process was the change in livery on Métro rolling stock. Coupled with the fact that the RATP was working to 'zero graffiti', a novel idea was adopted. This is quite simply applying a thin plastic film to the car body, in the chosen colours, which are easily cleaned or even replaced should they become damaged by graffiti. The MF77 trains on line 7 were the first to receive the new colours from the summer of 1992, followed by those on line 8. The trains on other lines followed suit and by 1996 all rolling stock was in the new colours, save for the MP55 trains on line 11 which retained their old colours, being scheduled for early withdrawal and thus retaining their old colours until the end, albeit later than intended. Even the unrefurbished trains of MP59 stock on line 4 received the new colours, similarly being destined for early scrapping, now expected to be completed during 1999. Although the process of applying the protective film could be done far quicker than a full repaint, it was possible to see trains in different liveries side by side during the transition period.

Another aspect of the new corporate identity was in the signage at stations, not only in the *direction* and *correspondance* signs, but for station names and line diagrams. Each line has been given its own colour identity which can be identified with the line number.

New signs were trialled from May 1994 at Château de Vincennes on line 1 and at Place d'Italie from January 1995, along with a newly designed ticket office at the former. The new tri-lingual platform signs incorporate specifically numbered exits which relate to the exits indicated on the Plan du Quartier, an idea taken from the Tokyo subway system. The station name signs were replaced using the standard white-on-blue style, but in lower case lettering. Stations fitted with new signs with a name suffix have this in white on brown. It is currently planned that resigning of the Métro system will be done when other station work gives this opportunity.

Although the service reliability of the Paris Métro is to be envied by many other transport operators, in 1998 the RATP nevertheless experimented in train indicators, showing the time the next trains were expected to arrive. On the eastbound platform at Havre-Caumartin on line 3, the simplicity of end-to-end running is shown, with all trains destined for Pont de Levallois. *Brian Hardy*

On line 13, which has two northern branches of unequal length, an indicator was trialled on the northbound platform at Place de Clichy which showed the first two trains to each destination. *Brian Hardy*

Train Formations

Train formations are normally listed in the numerical order of the centre (former first class) car, which is also used to identify the location of stabled trains on the (normally green) chalk boards at train staff booking-on points and stabling areas. On many stocks, the car number, or part of it, can be found underneath the driving cab windows. 'G' suffix indicates that the train has rail greasing equipment fitted. Formations on some lines may, from time to time, be changed.

LINE 1
30x6-CAR TRAINS – TYPE MP59 – REFURBISHED 1990–1992

Note – These trains will be transferred to line 4 during 1999.

3131	4071	6004	5559	4108	3042
3111	4027	6005	5543	4046	3078
3049	4055	6006	5534	4022	3090
3081	4045	6007	5518	4020	3054
3063	4047	6010	5549	4054	3044
3101	4039	6011	5522	4082	3104
3105	4101	6013	5525	4088	3046
3089	4089	6016	5542	4076	3130
3107	4033	6017	5551	4050	3040
3099	4019	6018	5523	4040	3108
3119	4067	6021	5538	4028	3128
3069	4107	6022	5560	4048	3082
3091	4037	6026	5528	4092	3056
3067	4029	6027	5550	4080	3114
3093	4079	6028	5558	4090	3118
3113	4025	6029	5530	4030	3060
3097	4099	6030	5537	4100	3112
3087	4065	6032	5540	4038	3050
3133	4035	6036	5527	4042	3062
3103	4021	6037	5554	4104	3064
3125	4115	6038	5541	4044	3134
3203	4087	6039	5553	4084	3058
3047	4083	6040	5536	4116	3086
3051	4063	6041	5544	4106	3120
3079	4093	6042	5539	4114	3120
3059	4113	6044	5520	4094	3098
3043	4041	6045	5526	4112	3074
3123	4057	6047	5545	4032	3072
3127	4091	6059	5576	4184	3202
3175	4157	6071	5533	4158	3176

Spare Car:
3065

Summary:

	M	N	A	B	Total
MP59A	53	52	27	29	161
MP59B	4	5	2	1	12
MP59C	4	3	1	—	8
Total:	**61**	**60**	**30**	**30**	**181**

MP89 STOCK – 52x6-CAR TRAINS

Train sets outstanding to enter service at the end of March 1999 are shown in italic.

89 S 001	89 N1 001	89 N2 001	89 N2 002	89 N1 002	89 S 002
89 S 003	89 N1 003	89 N2 003	89 N2 004	89 N1 004	89 S 004
89 S 005	89 N1 005	89 N2 005	89 N2 006	89 N1 006	89 S 006
89 S 007	89 N1 007	89 N2 007	89 N2 008	89 N1 008	89 S 008
89 S 009	89 N1 009	89 N2 009	89 N2 010	89 N1 010	89 S 010
89 S 011	89 N1 011	89 N2 011	89 N2 012	89 N1 012	89 S 012
89 S 013	89 N1 013	89 N2 013	89 N2 014	89 N1 014	89 S 014
89 S 015	89 N1 015	89 N2 015	89 N2 016	89 N1 016	89 S 016
89 S 017	89 N1 017	89 N2 017	89 N2 018	89 N1 018	89 S 018
89 S 019	89 N1 019	89 N2 019	89 N2 020	89 N1 020	89 S 020
89 S 021	89 N1 021	89 N2 021	89 N2 022	89 N1 022	89 S 022
89 S 023	89 N1 023	89 N2 023	89 N2 024	89 N1 024	89 S 024
89 S 025	89 N1 025	89 N2 025	89 N2 026	89 N1 026	89 S 026
89 S 027	89 N1 027	89 N2 027	89 N2 028	89 N1 028	89 S 028
89 S 029	89 N1 029	89 N2 029	89 N2 030	89 N1 030	89 S 030
89 S 031	89 N1 031	89 N2 031	89 N2 032	89 N1 032	89 S 032
89 S 033	89 N1 033	89 N2 033	89 N2 034	89 N1 034	89 S 034
89 S 035	89 N1 035	89 N2 035	89 N2 036	89 N1 036	89 S 036
89 S 037	89 N1 037	89 N2 037	89 N2 038	89 N1 038	89 S 038
89 S 039	89 N1 039	89 N2 039	89 N2 040	89 N1 040	89 S 040
89 S 041	89 N1 041	89 N2 041	89 N2 042	89 N1 042	89 S 042
89 S 043	89 N1 043	89 N2 043	89 N2 044	89 N1 044	89 S 044
89 S 045	89 N1 045	89 N2 045	89 N2 046	89 N1 046	89 S 046
89 S 047	89 N1 047	89 N2 047	89 N2 048	89 N1 048	89 S 048
89 S 049	89 N1 049	89 N2 049	89 N2 050	89 N1 050	89 S 050
89 S 051	89 N1 051	89 N2 051	89 N2 052	89 N1 052	89 S 052
89 S 053	89 N1 053	89 N2 053	89 N2 054	89 N1 054	89 S 054
89 S 055	89 N1 055	89 N2 055	89 N2 056	89 N1 056	89 S 056
89 S 057	89 N1 057	89 N2 057	89 N2 058	89 N1 058	89 S 058
89 S 059	89 N1 059	89 N2 059	89 N2 060	89 N1 060	89 S 060
89 S 061	*89 N1 061*	*89 N2 061*	*89 N2 062*	*89 N1 062*	*89 S 062*
89 S 063	*89 N1 063*	*89 N2 063*	*89 N2 064*	*89 N1 064*	*89 S 064*
89 S 065	*89 N1 065*	*89 N2 065*	*89 N2 066*	*89 N1 066*	*89 S 066*
89 S 067	*89 N1 067*	*89 N2 067*	*89 N2 068*	*89 N1 068*	*89 S 068*
89 S 069	*89 N1 069*	*89 N2 069*	*89 N2 070*	*89 N1 070*	*89 S 070*
89 S 071	*89 N1 071*	*89 N2 071*	*89 N2 072*	*89 N1 072*	*89 S 072*
89 S 073	*89 N1 073*	*89 N2 073*	*89 N2 074*	*89 N1 074*	*89 S 074*
89 S 075	*89 N1 075*	*89 N2 075*	*89 N2 076*	*89 N1 076*	*89 S 076*
89 S 077	*89 N1 077*	*89 N2 077*	*89 N2 078*	*89 N1 078*	*89 S 078*
89 S 079	*89 N1 079*	*89 N2 079*	*89 N2 080*	*89 N1 080*	*89 S 080*
89 S 081	*89 N1 081*	*89 N2 081*	*89 N2 082*	*89 N1 082*	*89 S 082*
89 S 083	*89 N1 083*	*89 N2 083*	*89 N2 084*	*89 N1 084*	*89 S 084*
89 S 085	*89 N1 085*	*89 N2 085*	*89 N2 086*	*89 N1 086*	*89 S 086*
89 S 087	*89 N1 087*	*89 N2 087*	*89 N2 088*	*89 N1 088*	*89 S 088*
89 S 089	*89 N1 089*	*89 N2 089*	*89 N2 090*	*89 N1 090*	*89 S 090*
89 S 091	*89 N1 091*	*89 N2 091*	*89 N2 092*	*89 N1 092*	*89 S 092*
89 S 093	*89 N1 093*	*89 N2 093*	*89 N2 094*	*89 N1 094*	*89 S 094*
89 S 095	*89 N1 095*	*89 N2 095*	*89 N2 096*	*89 N1 096*	*89 S 096*
89 S 097	*89 N1 097*	*89 N2 097*	*89 N2 098*	*89 N1 098*	*89 S 098*
89 S 099	*89 N1 099*	*89 N2 099*	*89 N2 100*	*89 N1 100*	*89 S 100*
89 S 101	*89 N1 101*	*89 N2 101*	*89 N2 102*	*89 N1 102*	*89 S 102*
89 S 103	*89 N1 103*	*89 N2 103*	*89 N2 104*	*89 N1 104*	*89 S 104*

LINE 2
47x5-CAR TRAINS – TYPE MF67E

10301	14301	13301	11301	10302
10303	14302	13302	11302	10304
10305	14303	13303	11303	10306
10307	14304	13304	11304	10308
10309	14305	13305	11305	10414
10311	14306	13306	11306	10312
10313	14307	13307	11307	10314
10315	14308	13308	11308	10316
10317	14309	13309	11309	10318
10319	14310	13310	11310	10320
10321	14311	13311	11311	10322
10323	14312	13312	11312	10324
10325	14313	13313	11313	10326
10327	14314	13314	11314	10328
10329	14315	13315	11315	10330
10331	14316	13316	11316	10332
10333	14317	13317	11317	10334
10335	14318	13318	11318	10336
10337	14319	13319	11319	10338
10339	14320	13320	11320	10340
10341	14321	13321	11321	10342
10349	14325	13325	11325	10350
10351	14326	13326	11326	10352
10353	14327	13327	11327	10354
10355	14328	13328	11328	10356
10357	14329	13329	11329	10358
10359	14330	13330	11330	10360
10361	14331	13331	11331	10362
10363	14332	13332	11332	10364
10365	14333	13333	11333	10366
10367	14334	13334	11334	10368
10369	14335	13335	11335	10370
10371	14336	13336	11336	10372
10373	14337	13337	11337	10374
10375	14338	13338	11338	10376
10377	14339	13339	11339	10378
10379	14340	13340	11340	10380
10381	14341	13341	11341	10382
10383	14342	13342	11342	10384
10385	14343	13343	11343	10386
10387	14344	13344	11344	10388
10389	14345	13345	11345	10390
10391	14346	13346	11346	10392
10393	14347	13347	11347	10394
10395	14348	13348	11348	10396
10397	14349	13349	11349	10413
10399	14350	13350	11350	10400

Spare Car:
10398

Summary:

	M	N	A	B	Total
Total:	95	47	47	47	**236**

LINE 3
45x5-CAR TRAINS – TYPE MF67A-D

10002	14156	12001	14153	10001
10011	14111	12011	14108	10012
10013	14115	12012	14120	10014
10015	14103	12013	14107	10016
10017	14031	12014	14060	10018
10019	14117	12015	14118	10020
10021	14013	12016	14014	10022
10023	14011	12017	14012	10203
10025	14113	12018	14112	10026
10027	14045	12019	14030	10028
10029	14109	12020	14110	10030
10031	14047	12021	14034	10032
10033	14059	12022	14054	10034
10035	14048	12023	14021	10036
10037	14049	12024	14020	10038
10039	14051	12025	14114	10040
10041	14050	12026	14037	10042
10043	14026	12027	14157	10044
10045	14127	12028	14128	10046
10047	14039	12029	14038	10048
10049	14043	12030	14042	10050
10219	11210	12043	11214	10220
10091	14017	12051	14044	10092
10093	14135	12052	14136	10094
10095	14155	12053	14032	10096
10097	14139	12054	14140	10098
10099	14105	12055	14106	10100
10101	14143	12056	14144	10102
10103	14061	12057	14036*	10104*
10105	14063	12058	14062	10106
10107	14151	12059	14152	10108
10109	14071	12060	14070	10110
10111	14083	12061	14082	10112
10113	14075	12062	14074	10114
10115	14079	12063	14078	10116
10117	14035	12064	14154	10118
10119	14087	12065	14086	10120
10121	14089	12066	14088	10122
10123	14097	12067	14096	10124
10125	14101	12068	14102	10126
10127	14099	12069	14098	10128
10129	14104	12070	14100	10130
10131	14145	12071	14146	10132
10133	14015	12072	14016	10134
10223	14158	13068	11121	10222

B14156 was ex-A13069   * Prototype refurbished cars.
B14157 was ex-A13067
B14158 was ex-A13061

Summary:

	M	NA	N	B	A	Total
MF67W1	2	1	—	—	—	3
MF67A1	36	20	—	—	—	56
MF67A2	—	1	—	—	—	1
MF67B1	3	—	—	—	—	3
MF67C1	44	22	1	—	—	67
MF67C2	5	—	2	—	—	7
MF67D	—	—	—	87	1	88
Total:	**90**	**44**	**3**	**87**	**1**	**225**

LINE 3bis
6x3-CAR TRAINS – TYPE MF67C-D
REFURBISHED 1997–1998

10215	14023	10216
10211	14046	10212
10209	14091	10210
10213	14092	10214
10217	14093	10218
10207	14142	10208

Summary:

	M	B	Total
MF67C2	12	—	12
MF67D	—	6	6
Total:	**12**	**6**	**18**

LINE 4
50x6-CAR TRAINS – TYPE MP59
(22 TRAINS REFURBISHED 1990–1992)

3232	4214	5591	6001	4213	3231	
3076	4096	5563	6002	4031	3037	R
3080	4098	5547	6003	4085	3077	R
3068	4102	5546	6008	4061	3071	R
3048	4036	5556	6009	4103	3057	R
3092	4060	5519	6012	4053	3039	R
3126	4068	5529	6014	4059	3055	R
3106	4120	5588	6015	4095	3117	R
3122	4066	5555	6019	4023	3053	R
3070	4062	5532	6020	4109	3129	R
3102	4078	5524	6023	4183	3201	R
3066	4026	5521	6024	4051	3109	R
3094	4072	5531	6025	4073	3085	R
3084	4024	5562	6031	4081	3061	R
3124	4110	5548	6033	4111	3121	R
3088	4056	5535	6034	4074	3045	R
3132	4064	5552	6035	4097	3083	R
3038	4070	5557	6043	4075	3115	R
3110	4086	5564	6046	4049	3213	R
3208	4190	5565	6048	4189	3207	
3096	4034	5566	6049	4119	3041	R
3222	4204	5568	6051	4203	3221	
3198	4180	5569	6052	4179	3197	
3158	4140	5570	6053	4197	3157	
3178	4128	5571	6054	4127	3177	
3196	4178	5572	6055	4177	3195	
3206	4148	5574	6056	4143	3161	
3172	4154	5577	6057	4153	3171	
3206	4188	5601	6058	4187	3205	
3166	4160	5600	6060	4147	3165	
3148	4130	5578	6061	4129	3147	
3146	4138	5579	6062	4159	3145	
3186	4168	5580	6063	4167	3185	
3154	4136	5589	6064	4135	3153	
3168*	4150	5582	6065	4149	3167*	
3224	4206	5607	6066	4205	3223	
3052	4052	5561	6067	4043	3095	R
3192	4174	5605	6074	4173	3191	
3204	4186	5599	6082	4185	3215	R
3116	4058	5575	6084	4105	3075	R
3234	4208	5608	6091	4207	3233	
3228	4210	5609	6092	4209	3227	
3230	4212	5610	6093	4211	3229	
3182	4164	5585	6094	4163	3181	
3226	4216	5612	6095	4215	3225	
3236	4218	5613	6096	4217	3235	
3238	4220	5614	6097	4219	3237	
3240	4222	5615	6098	4221	3239	
3136	4118	5586	6099	4117	3135	
3160	4142	5587	6100	4141	3159	

R - Refurbished train.
* Motor cars only refurbished.

Summary:

	M	N	A	B	Total
MP59A	38	38	19	17	112
MP59B	12	13	10	10	45
MP59C	34	33	11	16	94
MP59D	16	16	10	7	49
Total:	**100**	**100**	**50**	**50**	**300**

LINE 5
51x5-CAR TRAINS – TYPE MF67F

10501	11501	13501	14501	10502
10503	14502	13502	11502	10504
10505	14503	13503	11503	10506
10507	11504	13504	14504	10508
10509	14505	13505	11505	10510
10511	14506	13506	11506	10512
10513	14507	13507	11507	10514
10515	14508	13508	11508	10516
10517	14509	13509	11509	10518
10519	14510	13510	11510	10520
10521	14511	13511	11511	10522
10523	14512	13512	11512	10524
10525	14513	13513	11513	10526
10527	14514	13514	11514	10528
10529	14515	13515	11515	10603
10531	11516	13516	14516	10532
10533	11517	13517	14517	10534
10535	14518	13518	11518	10536
10537	14519	13519	11519	10538
10539	11520	13520	14520	10540
10541	14521	13521	11521	10542
10543	14522	13522	11522	10544
10545	14523	13523	11523	10546
10547	14524	13524	11524	10548
10549	14525	13525	11525	10550
10551	14526	13526	11526	10552
10553	14527	13527	11527	10554
10555	14528	13528	11528	10556
10557	14529	13529	11529	10558
10559	14530	13530	11530	10604
10561	14531	13531	11531	10562
10563	11532	13532	14532	10564
10565	14533	13533	11533	10566
10567	14534	13534	11534	10568
10569	11535	13535	14535	10570
10571	14536	13536	11536	10572
10573	14537	13537	11537	10574
10575	11538	13538	14538	10576
10577	14539	13539	11539	10578
10579	14540	13540	11540	10580
10581	11541	13541	14541	10582
10583	11542	13542	14542	10584
10585	11543	13543	14543	10586
10587	14544	13544	11544	10588
10589	11545	13545	14545	10590
10591	11546	13546	14546	10592
10593	11547	13547	14547	10594
10595	14548	13548	11548	10596
10597	14549	13549	11549	10598
10599	14550	13550	11550	10600
10601	14551	13551	11551	10602

Spare Cars:
10530   10560

Summary:

	M	N	A	B	Total
Total:	104	51	51	51	**257**

LINE 6
43x5-CAR TRAINS – TYPE MP73

3501	7001	6501	4501	3502	
3505	7003	6503	4503	3506	
3597	7005	6505	4549	3598	
3595	7007	6507	4548	3596	
3515	7008	6508	4508	3516	
3517	7009	6509	4509	3518	
3519	7010	6510	4510	3520	
3521	7011	6511	4511	3522	
3523	7012	6512	4512	3601	
3525	7013	6513	4513	3526	
3527	7014	6514	4514	3528	R
3529	7015	6515	4515	3530	
3531	7016	6516	4516	3532	
3533	7017	6517	4517	3534	
3535	7018	6518	4518	3536	
3537	7019	6519	4519	3538	
3539	7020	6520	4520	3540	
3541	7021	6521	4521	3542	
3543	7022	6522	4522	3544	
3545	7023	6523	4523	3546	
3547	7024	6524	4524	3548	
3549	7025	6525	4525	3550	
3551	7026	6526	4526	3552	
3553	7027	6527	4527	3554	
3555	7028	6528	4528	3556	
3557	7029	6529	4529	3558	*
3559	7030	6530	4530	3560	
3561	7031	6531	4531	3562	
3563	7032	6532	4532	3564	
3565	7033	6533	4533	3566	R
3567	7034	6534	4534	3568	
3569	7035	6535	4535	3570	
3571	7036	6536	4536	3572	
3573	7037	6537	4537	3574	
3575	7038	6538	4538	3576	
3577	7039	6539	4539	3578	
3579	7040	6540	4540	3580	
3583	7042	6542	4542	3584	
3585	7043	6543	4543	3586	
3587	7044	6544	4544	3588	
3589	7045	6545	4545	3590	
3591	7046	6546	4546	3592	R
3593	7047	6547	4547	3594	

* Prototype refurbishment by RATP.
R – First production refurbished trains.

Spare Cars:

3503	3510	4502	6502	7041
3504	3524	4504	6549	7047
3507	3581	4505		7049
3508	3582	4541		
3509	3602			

Summary:

	M	N	A	B	Total
MP73A	95	47	45	46	233
MP73P1	1	—	—	—	1
Total:	96	47	45	46	**234**

LINE 7
74x5-CAR TRAINS - TYPE MF77

30025	32025	31013	32026	30026
30027	32027	31014	32028	30028
30045	32045	31023	32046	30046
30047	32047	31024	32048	30048
30049	32049	31025	32050	30050
30051	32051	31026	32052	30052
30053	32053	31027	32054	30054
30057	32057	31029	32058	30058
30059	32059	31030	32060	30060
30061	32061	31031	32062	30062
30063	32063	31032	32064	30064
30065	32065	31033	32066	30066
30067	32067	31034	32068	30068
30069	32069	31035	32070	30070
30071	32071	31036	32072	30072
30073	32073	31037	32074	30074
30075	32075	31038	32076	30076
30077	32077	31039	32078	30078
30079	32079	31040	32080	30080
30081	32081	31041	32082	30082
30101	32101	31051	32102	30102
30103	32103	31052	32104	30104
30105	32105	31053	32106	30106
30107	32107	31054	32108	30108
30109	32109	31055	32110	30110
30111	32111	31056	32112	30112
30119	32119	31060	32120	30120
30121	32121	31061	32122	30122
30123	32123	31062	32124	30124
30159	32159	31080	32160	30160
30161	32161	31081	32162	30162
30163	32163	31082	32164	30164
30165	32165	31083	32166	30166
30167	32167	31084	32168	30168
30169	32169	31085	32170	30170
30171	32171	31086	32172	30172
30177	32177	31089	32178	30178
30179	32179	31090	32180	30180
30181	32181	31091	32182	30182
30183	32183	31092	32184	30184
30187	32187	31094	32188	30188
30189	32189	31095	32190	30190
30191	32191	31096	32192	30192
30229	32229	31115	32230	30230
30293	32293	31147	32294	30294
30317	32317	31159	32318	30318
30319	32319	31160	32320	30320
30321	32321	31161	32322	30322
30323	32323	31162	32324	30324
30325	32325	31163	32326	30326
30327	32327	31164	32328	30328
30329	32329	31165	32330	30330
30331	32331	31166	32332	30332
30333	32333	31167	32334	30334
30335	32335	31168	32336	30336
30337	32337	31169	32338	30338
30339	32339	31170	32340	30340
30341	32341	31171	32342	30342
30343	32343	31172	32344	30344
30345	32345	31173	32346	30346
30347	32347	31174	32348	30348
30349	32349	31175	32350	30350
30351	32351	31176	32352	30352
30353	32353	31177	32354	30354
30355	32355	31178	32356	30356
30357	32357	31179	32358	30358
30359	32359	31180	32360	30360
30361	32361	31181	32362	30362
30363	32363	31182	32364	30364
30365	32365	31183	32366	30366
30367	32367	31184	32368	30368
30369	32369	31185	32370	30370
30371	32371	31186	32372	30372
30373	32373	31187	32374	30374

Summary:

	M	NA	B	Total
Total:	148	74	148	**370**

LINE 7bis
9x3-CAR TRAINS – TYPE MF88

88 M 001	88 B 001	88 M 002
88 M 003	88 B 002	88 M 004
88 M 005	88 B 003	88 M 006
88 M 007	88 B 004	88 M 008
88 M 009	88 B 005	88 M 010
88 M 011	88 B 006	88 M 012
88 M 013	88 B 007	88 M 014
88 M 015	88 B 008	88 M 016
88 M 017	88 B 009	88 M 018

Summary:

	M	B	Total
Total:	18	9	**27**

LINE 8
60x5-CAR TRAINS – TYPE MF77

30003	32003	31002	32004	30004	30233	32333	31117	32234	30234
30029	32029	31015	32030	30030	30235	32335	31118	32236	30236
30031	32031	31016	32032	30032	30237	32237	31119	32238	30238
30033	32033	31017	32034	30034	30239	32239	31120	32240	30240
30035	32035	31018	32036	30036	30241	32241	31121	32242	30242
30039	32039	31020	32040	30040	30243	32243	31122	32244	30244
30083	32083	31042	32084	30084	30245	32245	31123	32246	30246
30085	32085	31043	32086	30086	30247	32247	31124	32248	30248
30087	32087	31044	32088	30088	30249	32249	31125	32250	30250
30173	32173	31087	32174	30174	30251	32251	31126	32252	30252
30175	32175	31088	32176	30176	30253	32253	31127	32254	30254
30185	32185	31093	32186	30186	30255	32255	31128	32256	30256
30193	32193	31097	32194	30194	30257	32257	31129	32258	30258
30195	32195	31098	32196	30196	30259	32259	31130	32260	30260
30197	32197	31099	32198	30198	30261	32261	31131	32262	30262
30199	32199	31100	32200	30200	30263	32263	31132	32264	30264
30201	32201	31101	32202	30202	30265	32265	31133	32266	30266
30203	32203	31102	32204	30204	30267	32267	31134	32268	30268
30205	32205	31103	32206	30206	30269	32269	31135	32270	30270
30207	32207	31104	32208	30208	30271	32271	31136	32272	30272
30209	32209	31105	32210	30210	30273	32273	31137	32274	30274
30211	32211	31106	32212	30212	30275	32275	31138	32276	30276
30213	32213	31107	32214	30214	30277	32277	31139	32278	30278
30215	32215	31108	32216	30216	30279	32279	31140	32280	30280
30217	32217	31109	32218	30218	30281	32281	31141	32282	30282
30219	32219	31110	32220	30220	30283	32283	31142	32284	30284
30223	32223	31112	32224	30324	30285	32285	31143	32286	30286
30225	32225	31113	32226	30326	30287	32287	31144	32288	30288
30227	32227	31114	32228	30328	30289	32289	31145	32290	30290
30231	32331	31116	32232	30332	30291	32291	31146	32292	30292

Summary:

	M	NA	B	Total
Total:	120	60	120	300

LINE 9
72x5-CAR TRAINS – TYPE MF67A-D: 16 trains S-N-NA-N-S, 56 trains M-N-A-B-M
70 TRAINS REFURBISHED 1995–1998

9149	11153	12037	11174	9150		10135	14126	13031	11136	10136
9103	11079	12040	11145	9076		10137	14129	13032	11138	10138
9114	11088	12041	11082	9124		10139	14058	13033	11140	10140
9073	11147	12079	11173	9101		10141	14131	13034	11142	10142
9146	11054	12080	11165	9085		10143	14132	13035	11144	10144
9123	11203	12086	11230	9157		10187	14040	13036	11164	10164
9147	11157	12087	11161	9105		10147	14041	13037	11148	10148
9015	11232	12088	11220	9016		10149	14133	13038	11150	10150
9086	11209	12091	11207	9116		10151	14134	13039	11166	10152
9107	11149	12104	11151	9083		10153	14150	13040	11154	10154
9046	11189	12107	11167	9129		10155	14149	13041	11156	10156
9132	11217	12108	11219	9151		10157	14029	13042	11158	10158
9059	11233	12110	11205	9060		10159	14076	13043	11160	10160
9042	11169	12111	11179	9136		10161	14138	13044	11162	10162
9045	11086	12126	11229	9054		10145	14084	13045	11146	10146
9167	11159	12128	11234	9130*		10167	14141	13046	11168	10168
10051	14018	13011	11052	10052		10165	14147	13047	11152	10166
10053	11155	13012	14033	10083		10055	11170	13048	14123	10056
10087	14019	13013	11081	10088		10171	14027	13049	11172	10172
10070	14024	13014	11058	10064		10173	14095	13050	11197	10174
10067	11060	13015	14022	10068		10175	14130	13051	11190	10202
10061	11062	13016	14094	10062		10177	14077	13052	11178	10178
10063	14124	13017	11064	10058		10179	14122	13053	11180	10180
10065	14025	13018	11066	10066		10181	14121	13054	11182	10182
10059	11068	13019	14137	10060		10183	14085	13055	11184	10199
10069	14056	13020	11070	10072		10185	14055	13056	11186	10186
10071	14067	13021	11072	10054		10163	11188	13057	14052	10188
10073	14066	13022	11074	10074		10189	11176	13058	14065	10176
10191	11192	13023	14116	10192		10076	14053	13059	11076	10084
10077	14069	13024	11078	10078		10197	14028	13062	11198	10198
10079	14073	13025	11080	10080		10200	14064	13063	11200	10184
10081	11051	13026	11082	10082		10201	14080	13064	11202	10190
10085	14068	13027	11056	10086		10224	14081	13065	11204	10204
10075	11084	13028	14119	10057		10205	14090	13066	11206	10206
10169	14057	13029	11221	10170		10195	14148	13071	11196	10196
10089	14125	13030	11090	10090		10005	14159	13073	11006	10006*

Spare Car:
13070

* Non-refurbished trains.
A13073 was ex-NA12003
B14159 was ex-N11005
S9167 was ex-M10310

Summary:

	M	N	NA	A	B	S	Total
MF67A2	39	22	3	—	—	—	64
MF67B2	1	1	—	—	—	—	2
MF67C2	70	59	11	—	—	—	140
MF67C2A	2	1	—	1	1	—	5
MF67CX	—	5	2	—	—	—	7
MF67D	—	—	—	56	55	31	142
MF67E	—	—	—	—	—	1	1
Total:	112	88	16	57	56	32	361

LINE 10
30x5-CAR TRAINS:
21x5-CAR TRAINS – TYPE MF67A-D AND
9x5-CAR TRAINS – TYPE MF67E

9074	11213	11212	11228	9041
9113	11067	12033	11143	9068
9029	11183	12039	11089	9053
9092	11141	12046	11137	9148
9063	11075	12047	11069	9152
9164	11163	12048	11171	9154
9091	11224	12050	11222	9070
9030	11201	12077	11195	9156
9110	11059	12082	11199	9131
9102	11177	12084	11181	9141
9017	11187	12092	11175	9158
9166	11211	12096	11139	9087
9039	11087	12101	11193	9022
9090	11227	12109	11208	9089
9058	11135	12112	11185	9024
9165	11215	12113	11191	9075
9018	11231	12114	11065	9019
9078	11061	12115	11073	9071
9155	11077	12122	11057	9081
9088	11083	12124	11085	9072
9033	11071	12125	11223	9034
10344	14322	13322	11322	10343
10346	14323	13323	11323	10345
10348	14324	13324	11324	10347
10401	14351	13351	11351	10402
10403	14352	13352	11352	10404
10405	14353	13353	11353	10406
10407	14354	13354	11354	10408
10409	14355	13355	11355	10410
10411	14356	13356	11356	10412

Summary:

	M	N	NA	A	B	S	Total
MF67A2	—	14	6	—	—	—	20
MF67C2	—	27	11	—	—	—	38
MF67CX	—	2	3	—	—	—	5
MF67D	—	—	—	—	—	42	42
MF67E	18	9	—	9	9	—	45
Total:	**18**	**52**	**20**	**9**	**9**	**42**	**150**

LINE 11
20x4-CAR TRAINS – TYPE MP59B-C (REFURBISHED 1994-1995)
3x4-CAR TRAINS – TYPE MP73/86

MP59 STOCK:

3188	6050	4175	3187
3212	6068	4169	3211
3156	6069	4137	3155
3140	6070	4121	3139
3190	6072	4171	3189
3180	6073	4161	3179
3220	6075	4201	3219
3138	6076	4195	3164
3210	6077	4191	3209
3218	6078	4155	3217
3194	6079	4199	3193
3214	6080	4145	3216
3200	6081	4181	3199
3142	6083	4123	3141
3152	6085	4133	3151
3144	6086	4193	3143
3174	6087	4125	3173
3170	6088	4151	3169
3150	6089	4131	3149
3184	6090	4165	3183

MP73/86 STOCK:

3511	6506	4506	3512
3513	6548	4507	3514
3599	7006	7050	3600

Summary:

	M	N	A	B	Total
MP59B	13	6	1	—	20
MP59C	27	14	19	—	60
MP73A	4	2	2	1	9
MP73P2	—	—	—	1	1
MP86	2	—	—	—	2
Total:	**46**	**22**	**22**	**2**	**92**

LINE 12
42x5-CAR TRAINS - TYPE MF67A-D:

9100	11027	12031	11020	9057
9095	11092	12032	11037	9061
9021	11112	12034	11115	9020
9112	11025	12035	11029	9119
9118	11122	12036	11111	9108
9077	11013	12038	11015	9145
9051	11018	12042	11127	9121
9140	11030	12044	11091	9120
9043	11216	12045	11063	9142
9109	11031	12049	11023	9035
9096	11028	12073	11096	9094
9038	11055	12074	11053	9056
9044	11046	12075	11012	9162
9111	11044	12076	11039	9012
9117	11014	12078	11017	9115
9144	11033	12081	11019	9143
9036	11021	12083	11042	9062
9093	11123	12085	11093	9050
9122	11016	12089	11041	9134
9127	11022	12090	11109	9128
9106	11129	12093	11124	9055
9082	11106	12094	11128	10024
9125	11103	12095	11101	9025
9031	11100	12097	11095	9037
9032	11114	12098	11034	9066
9026	11118	12099	11040	9160
9049	11043	12100	11117	9133
9052	11102	12102	11104	9013
9080	11048	12103	11113	9023
9138	11032	12105	11026	9163
9069	11110	12106	11119	9098
9014	11001	12116	11116	9126
9064	11002	12117	11125	9161
9048	11098	12118	11120	9047
9137	11099	12120	11105	9065
9153	11130	12121	11047	9028
9139	11036	12123	11045	9027
9104	11011	12127	11094	9084
9040	11049	12129	11035	9135
9079	11050	12130	11024	9097
9159	11038	12131	11126	9099
9067	11097	12132	11108	9011

Spare Car:
11107

NA 12129 was ex-N11131
NA 12131 was ex-N11133
NA 12130 was ex-N11132
NA 12132 was ex-N11134

Summary:

	M	N	NA	S	Total
MF67W1	—	2	—	—	2
MF67A1	—	40	—	—	40
MF67A2	—	3	10	—	13
MF67B1	1	—	—	—	1
MF67C1	—	39	4	—	43
MF67C2	—	1	24	—	25
MF67CX	—	—	4	—	4
MF67D	—	—	—	83	83
Total:	**1**	**85**	**42**	**83**	**211**

LINE 13
62x5-CAR TRAINS - TYPE MF77

30001	32001	31001	32002	30002		30141	32141	31071	32142	30142
30010	32006	31003	32005	30006		30143	32143	31072	32144	30144
30007	32007	31004	32008	30008		30145	32145	31073	32146	30146
30009	32009	31005	32010	30005		30147	32147	31074	32148	30148
30011	32011	31006	32012	30012		30149	32149	31075	32150	30150
30013	32014	31007	32013	30014		30151	32151	31076	32152	30152
30015	32016	31008	32015	30016		30137	32137	31077	32153	30153
30017	32017	31009	32018	30018		30155	32155	31078	32156	30156
30019	32020	31010	32019	30020		30157	32157	31079	32158	30158
30021	32021	31011	32022	30022		30221	32221	31111	32222	30222
30023	32024	31012	32023	30024		30295	32295	31148	32296	30296
30037	32037	31019	32038	30038		30297	32297	31149	32298	30298
30041	32041	31021	32042	30042		30299	32299	31150	32300	30300
30043	32043	31022	32044	30044		30301	32301	31151	32302	30302
30055	32056	31028	32055	30056		30303	32303	31152	32304	30304
30089	32089	31045	32090	30090		30305	32305	31153	32306	30306
30091	32091	31046	32092	30092		30307	32307	31154	32308	30308
30093	32093	31047	32094	30094		30309	32309	31155	32310	30310
30095	32095	31048	32096	30096		30311	32311	31156	32312	30312
30097	32097	31049	32098	30098		30313	32313	31157	32314	30314
30099	32099	31050	32100	30100		30315	32315	31158	32316	30316
30113	32113	31057	32114	30114		30375	32375	31188	32376	30376
30115	32115	31058	32116	30116		30377	32377	31189	32378	30378
30117	32117	31059	32118	30118		30379	32379	31190	32380	30380
30125	32125	31063	32126	30126		30381	32381	31191	32382	30382
30127	32127	31064	32128	30128		30383	32383	31192	32384	30384
30129	32129	31065	32130	30130		30385	32385	31193	32386	30386
30131	32131	31066	32132	30132		30387	32387	31194	32388	30388
30133	32133	31067	32134	30134		30389	32389	31195	32390	30390
30135	32135	31068	32136	30136		30391	32391	31196	32392	30392
30139	32139	31070	32140	30140		30393	32393	31197	32394	30394

Spare cars:
31038
32138
31069

Summary:

	M	NA	B	Total
Total:	125	63	125	**313**

LINE 14
MP89 STOCK – 21x6-CAR TRAINS

89 S 1001	89 N1 1001	89 N2 1001	89 N2 1002	89 N1 1002	89 S 1002
89 S 1003	89 N1 1003	89 N2 1003	89 N2 1004	89 N1 1004	89 S 1004
89 S 1005	89 N1 1005	89 N2 1005	89 N2 1006	89 N1 1006	89 S 1006
89 S 1007	89 N1 1007	89 N2 1007	89 N2 1008	89 N1 1008	89 S 1008
89 S 1009	89 N1 1009	89 N2 1009	89 N2 1010	89 N1 1010	89 S 1010
89 S 1011	89 N1 1011	89 N2 1011	89 N2 1012	89 N1 1012	89 S 1012
89 S 1013	89 N1 1013	89 N2 1013	89 N2 1014	89 N1 1014	89 S 1014
89 S 1015	89 N1 1015	89 N2 1015	89 N2 1016	89 N1 1016	89 S 1016
89 S 1017	89 N1 1017	89 N2 1017	89 N2 1018	89 N1 1018	89 S 1018
89 S 1019	89 N1 1019	89 N2 1019	89 N2 1020	89 N1 1020	89 S 1020
89 S 1021	89 N1 1021	89 N2 1021	89 N2 1022	89 N1 1022	89 S 1022

89 S 1023	89 N1 1023	89 N2 1023	89 N2 1024	89 N1 1024	89 S 1024
89 S 1025	89 N1 1025	89 N2 1025	89 N2 1026	89 N1 1026	89 S 1026
89 S 1027	89 N1 1027	89 N2 1027	89 N2 1028	89 N1 1028	89 S 1028
89 S 1029	89 N1 1029	89 N2 1029	89 N2 1030	89 N1 1030	89 S 1030
89 S 1031	89 N1 1031	89 N2 1031	89 N2 1032	89 N1 1032	89 S 1032
89 S 1033	89 N1 1033	89 N2 1033	89 N2 1034	89 N1 1034	89 S 1034
89 S 1035	89 N1 1035	89 N2 1035	89 N2 1036	89 N1 1036	89 S 1036
89 S 1037	89 N1 1037	89 N2 1037	89 N2 1038	89 N1 1038	89 S 1038

Summary (current total):

	S	N	Total
Total:	38	76	114

To be delivered:

| 89 S 1039 | 89 N1 1039 | 89 N2 1039 | 89 N2 1040 | 89 N1 1040 | 89 S 1040 |
| 89 S 1041 | 89 N1 1041 | 89 N2 1041 | 89 N2 1042 | 89 N1 1042 | 89 S 1042 |

CARS USED FOR INSTRUCTION & SPARE CARS NON-LINE SPECIFIC

10003	11002	12002	13060	14001
10004	11004	12004	13072	14002
10007	11007	12119		
10008	11008			
10193	11194			
10194	11218			
10221	11225			
10225				
10226				
10227				

Summary:

	M	N	NA	A	B	Total
MF67W1	—	—	—	—	1	1
MF67W2	2	2	1	—	1	6
MF67C1A	2	2	1	—	—	5
MF67C2	4	2	—	—	—	6
MF67CS	2	1	1	—	—	4
MF67D	—	—	—	2	—	2
Total:	**10**	**7**	**3**	**2**	**2**	**24**

ROLLING STOCK VEHICLES & TYPES

MA	Matériel Articulé
MP	Matériel Pneu
MF	Matériel Fer
E	Unit (Elément)
M	Driving motor 2nd class (Motrice avec loge, deuxième classe)
Bb	Second class trailer (Remorque deuxième classe) *
B	Second class trailer (Remorque deuxième classe)
Ab	First class trailer (Remorque première classe) *
A	First class trailer (Remorque première classe)
AB	Composite trailer (Remorque mixte)
N	Non-driving motor 2nd class (Motrice sans loge, deuxième classe)
NA	Non-driving motor 1st class (Motrice sans loge, première classe)
PLC	Plate-forme à loge de conduite
S	Driving trailer 2nd class (Remorque avec loge de conduite, deuxième classe)
Sp	Driving trailer 2nd class with emergency driving desk only
VMI	Véhicule de Maintenance des Infrastructure (which includes all the following):

	T	Works train driving motor (Tracteur)
	TA	Depot shunting driving motor (Tracteur d'Atelier)
	TMA	Battery locomotive (Tracteur à Marche Autonome)
	TNG	Tracteur Nouvelle Génération
	V	Miscellaneous vehicles (Véhicule auxilière)
	VX	Static miscellaneous vehicle (Véhicule Fixe)

Note * Sprague and Nord-Sud stock only.

ROLLING STOCK STATISTICS
(Dimensions in metres)

	MP59	MP73	MP89 Line 1	MP89 Line 14	MF67	MF77	MF88
Cars per train	6*	5	6	6	5†	5	3
DRIVING MOTOR CARS (M)							
Length over couplers	15.615	15.615	—	—	15.615	15.470	15.500
Maximum width	2.480	2.480	—	—	2.420	2.460	2.440
Height from top of rail	3.485	3.485	—	—	3.430	3.460	3.480
Seats	24	24	—	—	24	22	20
Tip-up seats	28	28	—	—	28	23	26
DRIVING TRAILERS (S)							
Length over couplers	—	—	15.380	15.380	15.615	—	—
Maximum width	—	—	2.448	2.448	2.420	—	—
Height from top of rail	—	—	3.471	3.471	3.430	—	—
Seats	—	—	18	24	24	—	—
Tip-up seats	—	—	15	12	28	—	—
TRAILERS (A, AB, B)							
Length over couplers	14.790	14.790	—	—	14.790	15.500	15.500
Maximum width	2.480	2.480	—	—	2.420	2.460	2.440
Height from top of rail	3.485	3.485	—	—	3.430	3.460	3.480
Seats	24	24	—	—	24	28	24
Tip-up seats	30	30	—	—	30	24	28
NON-DRIVING MOTORS (N, NA)							
Length over couplers	14.790	14.790	14.880	14.880	14.790	15.500	—
Maximum width	2.480	2.480	2.448	2.448	2.420	2.460	—
Height from top of rail	3.485	3.485	3.471	3.471	3.430	3.460	—
Seats	24	24	28	24	24	28	—
Tip-up seats	30	30	16	12	30	24	—
Maximum speed (kph)	70	70	80	80	80	100	80
Train length	90.390	75.600	90.280	90.280	75.600	77.440	46.500
Door opening width	1.300	1.300	1.650	1.650	1.300	1.575	1.576
Seats per train	144	120	148	144	120	128	64
Standing capacity per train	556	455	540	578	455	446	282
Total capacity per train	700	575	688	722	575	574	346
Train unloaded weight	126.4	111.2	140.0	140.0	115–119	121.5	74.2

* Four cars line 11.
† Three cars line 3bis.